Sharing Time

A Big Person/Little Person Project Book

Dedication

I dedicate this book to my husband,
Robert Cobb Miller,
who provided me with this opportunity,
then spent hours editing and typing the manuscript.
Helping me find the confidence to write this book
has been one of his most special gifts.
He is my mentor and the love of my life.

Sharing Time

A Big Person/Little Person Project Book

Kathy Leichliter Miller

TAB BOOKS Inc.
Blue Ridge Summit, PA

FIRST EDITION
FIRST PRINTING

Copyright © 1990 by TAB BOOKS Inc.
Printed in the United States of America

Library of Congress Cataloging in Publication Data

Miller, Kathy Leichliter.
    Sharing time : a big person/little person project book / by Kathy
Leichliter Miller.
        p.   cm.
    ISBN 0-8306-9256-8   ISBN 0-8306-3256-5 (pbk.)
    1. Handicraft. I. Title.
TT157.M48   1990   89-36607
745.5—dc20   CIP

TAB BOOKS Inc. offers software for sale. For information and a catalog, please
contact TAB Software Department, Blue Ridge Summit, PA 17294-0850.

Questions regarding the content of this book
should be addressed to:

    Reader Inquiry Branch
    TAB BOOKS Inc.
    Blue Ridge Summit, PA 17294-0214

Acquisitions Editor: Kimberly Tabor
Book Editor: Eileen P. Baylus
Production: Katherine Brown
Paperbound cover photograph: Susan Riley, Harrisonburg, Virginia

Book development coordinated by Ramsey & Associates.

Contents

Quick Reference Guide

Project	Time Required	Age Group	Page
Build a Box Playhouse	🕐 🕐	<u>2 3 4 5 6 7</u> 8 9 10 11 12	1
Paint a Magic Picture	🕐	<u>2 3 4 5 6 7</u> 8 9 10 11 12	9
Make Textured Paint and Paint a Picture	🕐	<u>2 3 4 5 6 7</u> 8 9 10 11 12	15
Make a Sack Mask	🕐	<u>2 3 4 5 6 7</u> 8 9 10 11 12	19
Make Finger Paints	🕐	<u>2 3 4 5 6 7</u> 8 9 10 11 12	27
Make a Falling Rain Picture	🕐	<u>2 3 4 5 6 7</u> 8 9 10 11 12	32

Project	Time Required	Age Group	Page
Make a Wind Pinwheel		<u>2 3 4 5 6 7 8 9 10</u> 11 12	89
Make a Spice Ring		2 3 <u>4 5 6 7 8 9 10 11 12</u>	93
Make a Macaroni Angel Ornament		2 3 <u>4 5 6 7 8 9 10</u> 11 12	97
Make a Musical Maraca		<u>2 3 4 5 6 7</u> 8 9 10 11 12	102
Make a Drum		<u>2 3 4 5 6 7 8 9</u> 10 11 12	107
Make a Musical Instrument: A Bucket Bass		2 3 <u>4 5 6 7</u> 8 9 10 11 12	111
Make a Ukulele		2 3 <u>4 5 6 7 8 9</u> 10 11 12	117
Make a Braided Yarn Belt		2 3 4 5 6 7 <u>8 9 10 11 12</u>	122
Make a Baby Toy: Spools on a String		2 3 4 <u>5 6 7</u> 8 9 10 11 12	126
Make a Papier-Mâché Hand Puppet	2 afternoons	2 3 4 <u>5 6 7 8 9 10</u> 11 12	132

Project	Time Required	Age Group	Page
Make a Puppet Stage	2 afternoons	2 3 4 <u>5 6 7</u> 8 9 10 11 12	138
Make a Family Message Board	(clock)	2 3 4 <u>5 6</u> 7 8 9 10 11 12	144
Make a Hexagonal Kite	(clock)	2 3 4 <u>5 6 7</u> 8 9 10 11 12	149
Make a Telephone Magnet	(clock)	2 3 4 <u>5 6 7 8 9</u> 10 11 12	155
Make a Walnut Strawberry	(clock)	2 3 4 <u>5 6 7</u> 8 9 10 11 12	159
Make a Scented Candle	(clock) (clock)	2 3 4 5 <u>6 7 8 9</u> 10 11 12	164
Make a Jigsaw Puzzle	weekend 2 afternoons	2 3 <u>4 5 6 7</u> 8 9 10 11 12	169
Make a Beautiful Daisy	(clock) (clock)	2 3 4 5 6 <u>7 8 9 10</u> 11 12	174
Make a Beautiful Leaf Plaque	(clock)	2 3 4 5 6 <u>7 8 9 10</u> 11 12	180
Make a Fancy Photograph Album	(clock)	2 3 4 5 6 <u>7 8 9 10</u> 11 12	185

Project	Time Required	Age Group	Page
Make a Kitchen or Closet Organizer	(one clock face)	2 3 4 5 6 <u>7 8 9 10 11 12</u>	191
Make a Rubber Band Shooter	(two clock faces)	2 3 4 <u>5 6 7 8 9 10 11 12</u>	195
Make a Bubble Gum Machine	weekend 2 afternoons	2 3 4 5 6 <u>7 8 9 10 11 12</u>	200
Make a Wooden Doll House	1 to 2 afternoons	2 3 <u>4 5 6 7 8 9 10 11 12</u>	205

Acknowledgments

Many people have helped create this book. Among those I wish to acknowledge and thank are my son, Brent A. Thiessen, who drew the original illustrations, and his friend, Bill Wilkinson, who spent many hours inking the artwork Brent produced.

Skippy also wishes to thank Brent for giving him life in this book. It was fun watching to see just what Skippy would do next.

I also wish to thank my talented brothers and sisters for their project contributions and for providing so many memories of times past. They are: JoAnn and Jim Ratzlaff, Norman and Jeanie Leichliter, Homer and Luanna Leichliter, and Phil and Dianna Leichliter. My mother and dad were also encouraging, giving me ideas by helping me remember things I had done myself or with my children.

My special thanks also goes to Dan Ramsey. Without Dan's guidance and trust, none of this would have been possible.

Thank you also goes to the Newton, Kansas, High School journalism department for taking pictures of the doll house and to Mary Anne Seifkes for posing. Thanks to Scott Thiessen, my 13-year-old son, for taking many of the pictures in the book, and to my son Garry and daughter Nikki and her friends Adam Levis and Andy, Adam, and Aaron Miller for working on the projects and posing for the pictures.

This book became a project in which my whole family shared, so actually it is the Robert C. Miller family project book.

Introduction

"Mommy, can I help?"

"Daddy, can I do that?"

To any busy parent, these are such familiar questions. When my children ask to share my time, my memories turn to the times when I was young.

Some of the most wonderful times of my childhood were spent sharing an hour or an afternoon with my mother or dad. Although the projects have long since worn out and fallen apart, the memories are lasting. Unfortunately, I am now often unable to find enough time to do something with the children I love, and planning a project seems to take as much time as doing it. Do you have the same problem?

Sharing Time offers 40 projects that are easy to make and fun to share with your young child, grandchild, niece or nephew, neighbor's child, a Big Brother/Big Sister friend, or someone you're babysitting. The projects are simple: making toys, pictures, puzzles, cards, gifts, and useful novelties (Fig. I-1). Each takes only a short time to complete, yet the time spent together will be remembered for years.

Many of these projects are traditional, memorable crafts that you might have done with someone while you were growing up. What better thing to share with your own children than some of your own memories of childhood? Each project offers a picture or drawing and description of the result, a list of tools and materials, notes about safety (indicated by a stop sign) and the amount of time needed for the project, and step-by-step illustrated procedures.

Note to Parents:

Working with children is one of the great joys of my life. Over the past 20 years, I have raised four children and run a licensed daycare center in my home. This experience has taught me that children learn

Fig. I-1. A few of the 40 projects you can build with the instructions in this book.

acceptance, self-worth, and confidence when an adult, parent, teacher, guardian, or older sibling spends time with the child doing things and praising the child for his accomplishments, great or small.

This book is written to encourage you to make things with, and for, your children.

Build A Box Playhouse

Age Group: 2 to 7
Time Required: 2 to 3 hours

The afternoon was quiet and relaxed. Then the children burst through the door. They were excited. A delivery truck had just brought an expensive new playhouse to the children next door. In the days that followed the delivery, my children talked about how wonderful it would be to have a playhouse just like the one next door.

Like most parents, I wanted my children to have the same play experiences as other children. My children loved crawling around, under, and through things. The playhouse next door provided those activities and gave the neighbor children a private get-away place that is so important for children.

How I wished I could order the very same playhouse for my children. I could not afford to do that, so I applied some motherly creativity to the situation. Why not build an appliance box playhouse?

An appliance box playhouse is an innovative way to have a playhouse without buying one or spending hours making complicated plans and buying expensive materials. A box playhouse is made from a sturdy and roomy major appliance box from any appliance store. Just add a little ingenuity. This enjoyable activity will help you and your children share a special time together. You will see things through your children's eyes for these few shared hours. Even though the playhouse began as an appliance box, your child will express joy and excitement after the project is complete.

Materials and Tools

◇ One sturdy cardboard appliance box
◇ Any appropriate cutting tool, such as a razor knife
◇ Colored markers or crayons

◇ Construction paper
◇ Pencil
◇ Yardstick or tape measure

Planning

Always begin with imagination. If more than one child is going to help with this project, encourage the children to work together on a drawing of the outside of their "dream house." You might suggest where their playhouse will have a door and windows. Will there be shutters? Your junior architects will love making sketches of their finished playhouse.

Getting the Box

You must get the box for the playhouse from an appliance store. Before going to get the appliance box, make sure you have all the tools and materials you need. You probably have everything you need at home (except the box) so, before buying anything, check around your house for required items such as markers or crayons. If necessary, make a list of items you will need to purchase.

Before leaving home, find some string, twine, rope, or a rubber tie-down cord to take in the car with you. An appliance box is large and if you do not have a pick-up, van, or other cargo carrier, you will have to put the box in your trunk. You will need something to hold that trunk lid tightly against the box.

To get a box, pile the kids into the car and go to any appliance store. Ask for a sturdy stove or refrigerator box like the one shown in Fig. 1-1. If the store has just received a shipment of appliances and several different boxes are available, allow your children to choose the box they want for their playhouse. Put the box in the trunk and secure the lid with the string, twine, rope, or rubber tie-down cord.

During the trip to the appliance store, you also can pick up any of the other items needed. Appliance boxes are large and cumbersome, so put the box in the children's play area as soon as you reach home.

Getting Started

When you are ready to begin, gather the tools, the materials, and—this is the most important ingredient—the design of the playhouse created by the children. Now, you're ready to "build" your playhouse.

First, examine your appliance box. Usually, one end has been cut open, leaving one or more cardboard flaps. You can leave the open end up or turn the appliance box upside down so that the open end is on the floor. Either way, you can fold the open flaps in, cut them off, and use the cardboard. If you turn the box over, you can leave them out and let them form the porch or small yards or flower gardens of the playhouse.

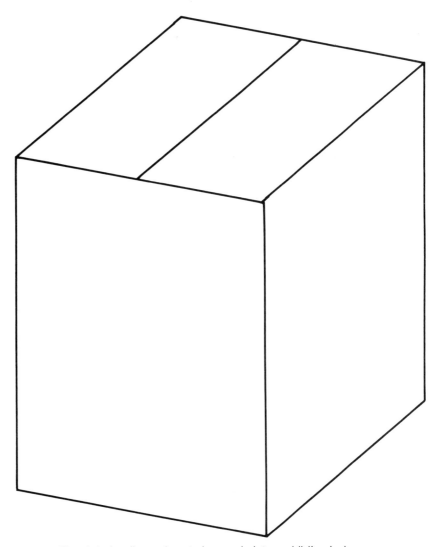

Fig. 1-1. Appliance box to be made into a child's playhouse.

Use the yardstick or tape measure to measure the tallest child who will be using the playhouse. Then, let the children draw the front door of the playhouse on the box. Show them how to use the yardstick or tape measure to draw a door large enough for the tallest child. You might suggest drawing the door on the narrower end of the box as shown in Fig. 1-2.

Now you must get involved. It is time to cut the door drawn by the children. Before starting to cut, show the children that a razor knife is sharp and slippery. Then, cut along the top, the side, and, if necessary, the bottom of the door drawing. In Fig. 1-2, the dashed lines indicate where to cut the cardboard box. Do not cut along the solid line.

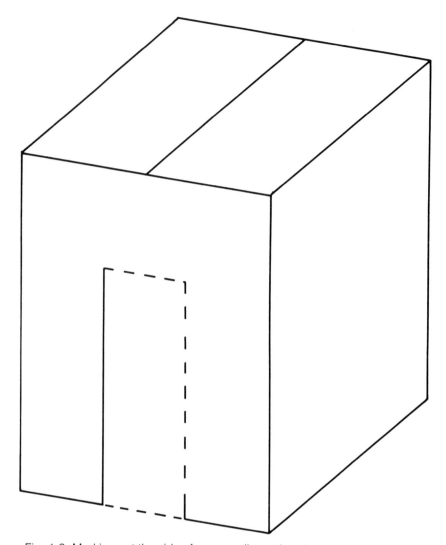

Fig. 1-2. Marking out the side of your appliance box for the playhouse door.

Because of the thickness of appliance box cardboard, you will need to make several deepening cuts along the lines drawn by the children. When you are finished, you should have an easy-to-open door (Fig. 1-3). If necessary, make a partial cut into the cardboard along the opposite side of the door so it will open and shut more easily. When this tough cutting job is finished, encourage your children to give you a word of compliment, a pat on the back, or a hug. You will be teaching them to show appreciation for a job well done.

Let the children finish drawing the design of the playhouse on the box. Cut windows and any other doors that the children have planned. Figure 1-4 shows a possible location for a playhouse window; Fig. 1-5 illustrates pride of ownership.

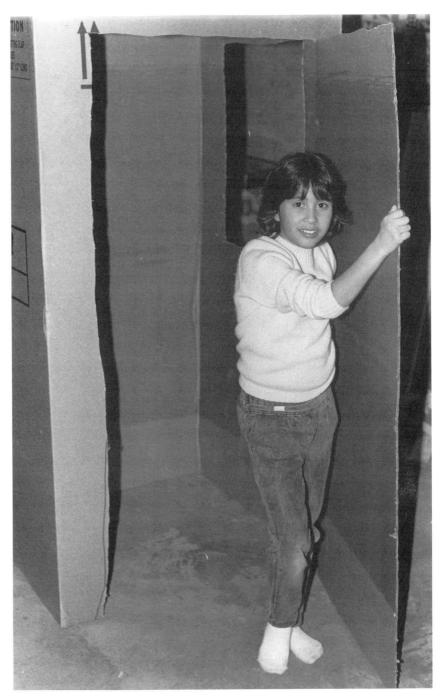

Fig. 1-3. Cut out the door carefully from the side of the appliance box.

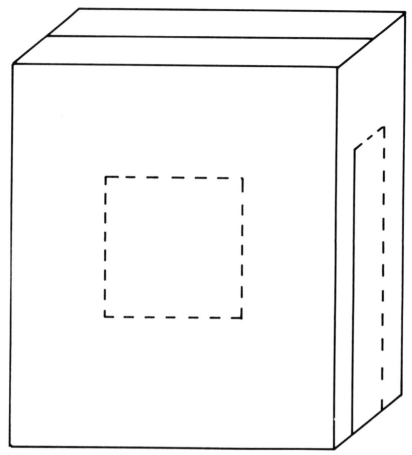

Fig. 1-4. Locating the playhouse window.

Finishing the Playhouse

Now, all the children can plunge into the fun. Let the children draw and color shutters, siding, or geometric designs on their playhouse.

Use construction paper to create additional decorations. A fringe of green construction paper glued around the bottom of the playhouse will look like grass. You can add flowers, too. Perhaps a flower box can decorate a window. Your children will want to add their own creative touches. Does your playhouse look like the one Skippy is enjoying in Fig. 1-6?

Only your children's imaginations will limit what you can do with a box playhouse. Why not make some curtains from inexpensive fabric? Add a cardboard "welcome" mat outside the front door. On an inside wall of the playhouse, draw a picture with an elegant frame. Have a house-warming party and send out invitations.

DO NOT DROP
OPPING WILL DAMAGE CONTENT
)TE: THIS PRODUCT WAS IN PERFECT CONDITION WHEN IT LEFT THE FACTORY. HOW
WE SUGGEST YOU CHECK THIS APPLIANCE FOR POSSIBLE APPARENT OR CONCEALEI
iE WHICH MAY HAVE OCCURRED IN TRANSIT. SAFE TRANSIT IS THE RESPONSIBILIT\
E CARRIER.

Fig. 1-5. Proud owner of a box playhouse.

In less than one afternoon, an exciting appliance box playhouse can
be completed. It is a simple, shared activity that allows you and your
children a chance to share ideas. Your children will learn about cooperation and you will have the chance to offer genuine praise for a job well
done. After it is finished, the playhouse provides an exciting, private
play place right in the corner of your children's bedroom or playroom.

Fig. 1-6. Skippy enjoys the completed box playhouse.

Project 2

Paint A
Magic Picture

Age Group: 2 to 7
Time Required: 2 hours

Any child is excited to watch something appear, as if by magic, from seemingly nothing. Children love projects that have an air of magic. In this project, your children will make a colorful design appear—as if by magic—from a black sheet of paper.

Most children enjoy coloring and painting activities, and this project provides that kind of fun, and more. This magic is a simple design scratched into a paint-covered crayon surface.

This project is perfect for those days when a child is somewhat listless and bored. You will know it is the right time for this project when a weak little voice pleadingly asks: "Isn't there anything I can do?" Now, you can say: "Yes, let's make a magic picture."

Instead of a bored and unhappy child, you will be creating a happy little person who will enjoy the time spent with you painting a magic picture. A magic picture relieves the boredom of bad weather or an otherwise unexciting day and creates lasting, loving memories of your time together.

The project also teaches important skills such as handling spoons and bowls, stirring, coloring, painting, and drawing. If several children work together, you can encourage sharing of colors and paint brushes. While the children are working, compliment each one of them. You will be setting a lasting example that they will remember when they become parents.

Get ready to have some fun making magic.

Materials and Tools

◇ Salt paint materials:
  • 2 teaspoons salt
  • 1 teaspoon water

- 3 drops black tempera paint
- 1 teaspoon liquid starch
◇ 9-×-12-inch white poster board for each magic picture
◇ Pencil
◇ Measuring spoon
◇ Several broad paintbrushes
◇ Small bowl for each child for mixing the paint
◇ Box of color crayons
◇ Newspapers
◇ Old clothing or a paint smock
◇ Several children who love to use crayons and paint

Gathering Materials and Getting Started

Gather your materials and find a comfortable place to work. The kitchen table is an excellent location because most of the materials you need are available in the kitchen. Cover the table with old newspapers just in case something spills.

Begin this project by making the salt paint. Does everyone have on old clothes? An adult's old shirt or blouse makes an excellent paint smock and children love wearing something that belonged to mom or dad.

Encourage your children to help you mix the salt paint. Even the smallest children are able to stir and pour with your help. Letting them get involved in preparing the paint helps them understand the importance of organization and preparation before beginning the actual process of creating something. If you are able to consistently teach organization and preparation before fun activities, you will see this same pattern carry over into daily work activities. Children will learn that things are much easier if they are organized and prepared for properly.

Put a small bowl on the table in front of each child and allow them to mix the ingredients for salt paint together. If the children are younger, you will want to measure out the various ingredients, but always let the children have the opportunity to try.

Remind the children not to taste the paint mixture. They will not be tempted to taste the mixture if you supervise mixing activities.

When the mixing activities have produced a deep, black paint, set the salt paint aside in a safe place where the paint bowl will not get bumped. Get ready for some vigorous coloring activity.

Create excitement by asking how many children really like to color. Everyone will volunteer. Give each child a piece of the white poster board and open the box of color crayons. Let each child choose several favorite colors. Tell the children to choose the colors they want to see in their magic picture. The colors that the children select and use are the source of charm in their magic pictures, so help them to choose bright colors.

While the children are picking colors, encourage them to share and be pleasant to one another.

Tell the children to make small patches of color all over the piece of white poster board just like Skippy is doing in Fig. 2-1. Children love this type of unstructured activity (Fig. 2-2). On the white poster board, there are no lines to get in the way of serious coloring. Give plenty of praise and encourage the children to cover the entire poster board. Do not leave any white space uncolored.

Fig. 2-1. Skippy begins his magic picture by making small patches of color on his white poster board.

This part of the activity will take the greatest amount of time. A 9-×-12-inch piece of poster board has a lot of white space to be colored. If the children get weary coloring the small patches all over the white poster board, don't be afraid to help them. Remember to ask if the colors you choose are their preference. After all, this is their magic picture.

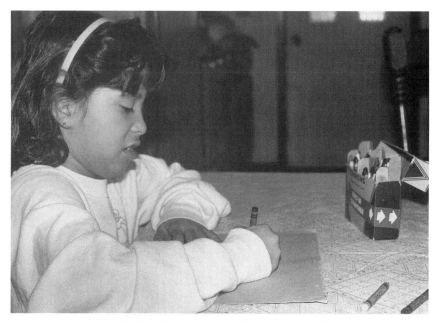
Fig. 2-2. Everybody helps make the magic picture.

After completing the coloring, it is time to use the salt paint. Give each child a paintbrush and have them paint the entire surface of the colored poster board with the black salt paint. Children love working with paint and a brush. See how much fun Skippy is having with the paint in Fig. 2-3. Just do not let the children get too messy. If necessary, make more salt paint. That's part of the fun.

The picture will appear totally black when they have finished. The process of covering their colored patches might alarm the children at first, but just explain the necessity of covering the surface so that, later, the magic picture can appear.

Drawing the Magic Picture

Allow the paint to dry for a few minutes. After the paint is dry, tell your children to get ready for some magic. Have each child begin to draw a picture into the surface of the paint with a pencil. Now, there is magic! Everywhere the child makes a pencil mark, a line of color will appear.

To reveal large areas of color, children can use the edge of a spoon to scratch off the black salt paint in larger areas (Fig. 2-4).

When your children have finished, a brightly colored picture will appear through the remaining areas of black paint (Fig. 2-5). The black paint will make the bright crayon colors even brighter.

Fig. 2-3. Skippy begins spreading the paint.

Fig. 2-4. The fun begins as black paint is scraped off with a spoon to reveal a unique design.

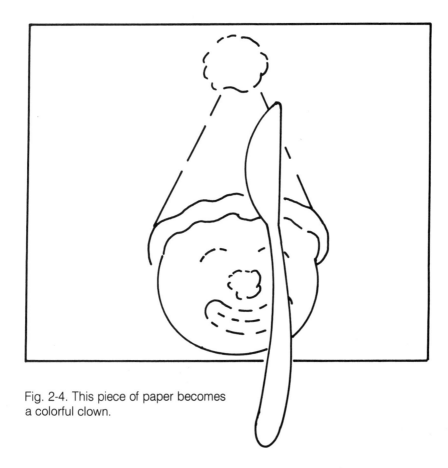

Fig. 2-4. This piece of paper becomes
a colorful clown.

Painting a magic picture allows your children to unleash their imaginations to create any design they desire. As they mark on their black poster boards, their favorite bright colors will appear. After this project is finished, plan to decorate bulletin boards, refrigerators, or bedroom walls with magic pictures.

Through a project such as this, your children will learn to develop their creative ideas. When you show excitement during the project and proudly display the results, you will be showing love and approval to the children. From these experiences, each child will grow to be more creative and loving.

Make Textured Paint And Paint A Picture

Age Group: 2 to 7

Time Required: 2 hours

Children love to paint. They are bold artists who daringly experiment with all kinds of color combinations. Now, when your children want to paint a picture, you can add a new dimension to their pictures: texture.

Most pictures are just plain old pictures made up of various shaped images and colors. However, with textured paint, your young artists will be able to paint pictures that are much more realistic. How would you like to actually experience your picture's shapes and contours? With textured paint, children can try painting a textured picture with sparkling snow, sandy deserts, or beautiful waves on an ocean. When children see such realism in a painting, creativity will be stimulated even more.

Textured paint is easy to make. In fact, the most valuable ingredient is your time to help the children mix ingredients and then use the paint. Making and using textured paint will encourage many important skills in your children: following directions, expressing creativity, sharing clean-up chores. Such skills are vital for school or at home.

Today, when your children come to you for something to do you can answer with excitement: "Let's paint a special picture. It will be a picture that you can touch and feel as well as see." A textured picture is just the thing for a special time together, just you and your children. Are you ready to begin?

Materials and Tools

◇ Textured paint:
  - 2 teaspoons salt
  - 1 teaspoon liquid starch
  - a few drops tempera paint for each color: brown, white, blue, yellow, and any other colors that are favorites of your children
  - 1 teaspoon of water

- ◇ Heavy, white paper such as white construction paper or poster paper: one piece for each textured painting
- ◇ Several small bowls or jars, one for each color of paint
- ◇ Measuring spoon
- ◇ Paintbrushes
- ◇ Tracing paper
- ◇ Tablecloth or newspapers
- ◇ Fine sand
- ◇ Colored glitter: silver, blue, red, etc.
- ◇ Pencil
- ◇ White glue

Getting Started—Mixing the Paint

Make sure your materials are available. Several important items might be difficult to find. You can find liquid starch at your grocery store or discount store. Fine sand is available in small bags from a hobby shop specializing in model railroad supplies.

Does the same hobby shop also have colored glitter? If not, try a craft shop. Now, you might ask, what's the difference between a craft shop and a hobby shop? Usually, a hobby shop is filled with plastic model kits, trains, games, toys, energetic children, and weary adults. A craft shop is the place to find things such as printer's boxes, miniature doll furniture, all sizes and shapes of Styrofoam, children looking bored, and eager adults.

Find a well-lighted work area. The kitchen table is a good place if you cover the table with a tablecloth or newspapers. Even the most careful child will occasionally have an accident and spill something or spread paint off the edge of the paper. When your work area is ready, begin mixing the textured paint.

Use one small bowl or jar for each color. Baby food jars with handy lids make excellent containers for mixing any type of paint. With a baby food jar, any leftover paint can be kept by putting the lid back on the jar.

First, try mixing one small bowl or jar of brown textured paint. Help your child measure the ingredients. Stir well to mix the ingredients and then add a small amount of fine sand. Let the children add the sand reminding them that too much sand will dry out the paint.

After mixing the brown textured paint, repeat the recipe and mix a bowl or jar of white, then blue, and next yellow. To the white paint, add silver glitter. If you were successful in finding other colors of glitter, add blue glitter to the blue paint and yellow glitter to the yellow paint.

Sketching a Picture

Have each child take a piece of white construction paper or poster paper. Encourage the children to sketch a simple picture, such as the examples shown in Figs. 3-1 and 3-2. Children ages 5 through 7 will want to copy the examples or try drawing one of their own.

Often, children will hesitate to draw an original picture. They will say: "I don't know what to draw." If children do not feel comfortable drawing a sketch on their own, you can sketch the picture for them and then let them paint it. Their picture might not turn out perfectly, but they will enjoy the process and the results, anyway.

If the children want to make a sketch but do not have that "just right" idea, you might suggest that the children place a piece of tracing paper over either Fig. 3-1 or Fig. 3-2 so they can easily copy either illustration. Then, show the children how to glue the tracing paper onto a sheet of white construction paper or poster paper. Now, the children can paint on the tracing paper.

Are you ready to begin painting? Let the children pick the colors to be used. A child's creativity, expressed in red skies and yellow water or in any other color scheme, is a wonderful thing. Your encouragement will help that creativity flourish.

Fig. 3-1. In the summertime, a snow scene is a fun sketch.

Fig. 3-2. During the winter, a warm beach scene can be drawn or traced.

If the children ask you for color suggestions, tell them to use the sandy brown paint for beaches and tree trunks. Use glittery white for snow, clouds, and whitecapped waves on the ocean. For an ocean and sky picture, suggest blue and then make either the blue water or blue sky a bit lighter by adding white to lighten the blue.

You can help your children experiment with different shades of color by doing such things as making the sky and the ocean different shades of blue. To complete a wonderful painting of the sea, add a yellow sun. Yellow is used only for the sun in the examples given here.

Let each picture dry completely before touching the different textures created by the sand and glitter in the paint. Show your children how proud you are by mounting each picture on a larger piece of poster board. Leave at least a 1-inch border around the picture.

Making and using textured paint adds a new dimension to the fun of painting a picture. Children will find new interest in painting when the paint makes a picture look so real. By helping your children with this project, you will be showing the children a lot of love and approval.

Have fun using your imagination and create a "see-and-touch" picture.

Project 4

Make A
Sack Mask

Age Group: 2 to 7

Time Required: 1 hour

Children enjoy wearing masks at any time of the year, even though Halloween is the traditional time to don a mask. My children loved to dress up and pretend. They also loved to cut, color, and experiment with construction paper, colored markers, scissors, and glue. Sack masks are fun to make because they can be as wild or funny as your children want them to be. Using your imagination is the key to having fun with sack masks.

Wearing a mask allows a child to try out different identities and experiment with different personalities. It is very important for a child to have this type of creative playtime, especially when the child plays with others. Valuable social skills are being learned here.

With a sack mask, a child can develop healthy play fantasies that will develop good social graces and a positive personality. Do not worry if a child sometimes takes on an angry or aggressive role in playtime. This is a normal way for a child to work through different feelings he or she might be experiencing.

While your children are working on their sack masks, you might relate to them a story where the character expresses positive behavior. Suggest that they imitate the character in their playtime.

A sack mask is a wonderful project for a variety of ages because it is so simple. It is just a brown paper grocery sack, decorated with colored markers and construction paper. The mask is inexpensive and a wonderful way to spend an hour with your children.

Materials and Tools

◇ 1 grocery sack for each mask
◇ Several different colored sheets of construction paper
◇ Cotton balls

◇ Glue
◇ Blunt scissors
◇ Colored markers
◇ Transparent tape
◇ Glitter or other decorations

Begin with Imagination

While you and your children are gathering your materials, begin discussing the type of masks you will be making. There are so many different masks that you can make.

Is it February? Make an Abraham Lincoln mask for a school program or history lesson. Around the Fourth of July, make an "Uncle Sam" mask with lots of puffy white cotton for a beard. At Christmas, make a Santa Claus mask. Yellow and brown construction paper can be used to create a lion's face while green construction paper can be cut and colored to make a whimsical alligator face.

Take the time to sit and talk about different ideas for a mask design. For each child, you could even draw some crude pictures of your children's ideas.

To use any of the designs shown here, lay tracing paper on the page and help your children trace the designs they would like to use. After the designs are traced, ask your children to cut them out. Children ages two and three will need your help to trace and cut the designs.

Share these ideas with your children and then let them decide what type of mask to make.

When each child has decided on a design, allow the children to choose the colors of construction paper and other materials needed for each of the masks.

Lay the designs on the construction paper. Ask the children to draw around each design to transfer the designs to the different colored construction paper.

Cutting Eyeholes and a Mouth

Now, give each child a grocery sack and have them put the sacks over their heads. This should cause excitement. With a grocery sack in place on each child's head, determine where the holes for the eyes and mouth should be just like in Fig. 4-1.

Use a crayon or colored marker and mark the location of the eyes and mouths with an X. Then, have each child remove the sack.

Draw the mouth on the designated place in whatever shape the child wants. Draw the eyes and nose, too. Use a pencil so the lines are only a pattern for cutting.

The children will enjoy cutting out the mouth and eyes (Fig. 4-2). Tell them to cut carefully along the pencil lines as Skippy is doing in Fig. 4-3. Stand by to apply some transparent tape if the scissors go too far or if the sack tears.

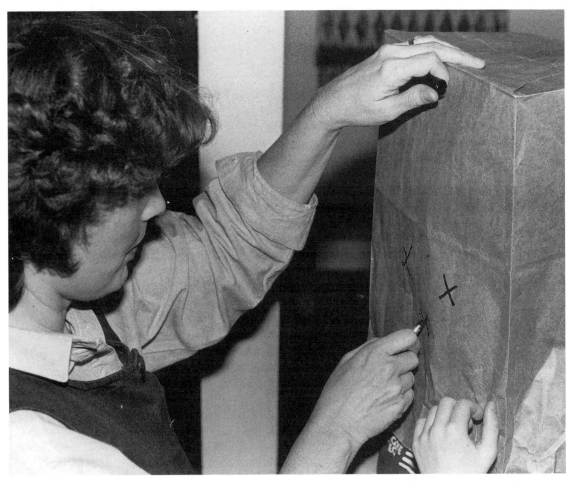

Fig. 4-1. Carefully mark location of the eyes on the grocery sack with a marker, *not* a sharp pencil.

Colored markers are good creative tools. Use them to color around the mouth or put a splash of extra color here and there on the mask.

Let the children glue on the eyebrows, eyelashes, mustache, hair, or any other facial features they have chosen from the examples in Figs. 4-4 and 4-5. Allow your children as much free expression as possible while they design the mask. When a great deal of the design is their idea, they are very enthusiastic and it helps build their self-esteem (Fig. 4-6).

A completed sack mask is shown in Fig. 4-7.

When the sack mask is completed, the children will be thrilled. Now, each of your children has an imaginative mask suitable for Halloween or any other occasion for playtime fun.

I remember the wonderful times that I spent with my own children helping them make sack masks for playtime fun and for use at school.

Fig. 4-2. Blunt scissors are used to cut out the marked holes.

My favorite part of the designing process was watching the delighted expressions of my children. The more I encouraged their efforts, the more elaborate the designs became. I could sense their feelings of accomplishment. Such experiences are so valuable for young children. In addition to the practice of basic skills such as tracing, coloring, and cutting, children making sack masks learn to appreciate themselves and value their own creativity.

Fig. 4-3. Skippy enjoys cutting big holes in the bag for his eyes and mouth.

Fig. 4-4. Who would recognize your child with one of these mustaches?

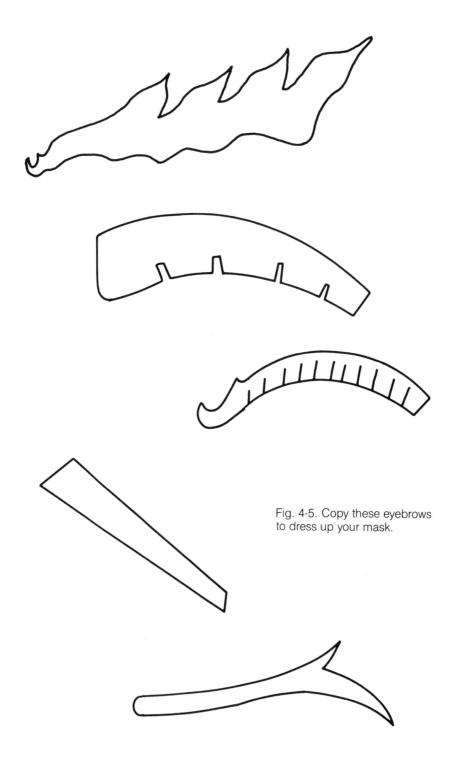

Fig. 4-5. Copy these eyebrows
to dress up your mask.

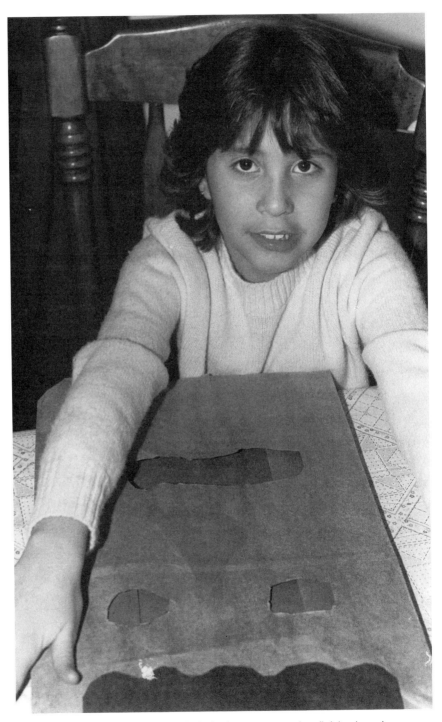

Fig. 4-6. This child has included a large nose on her finished mask.

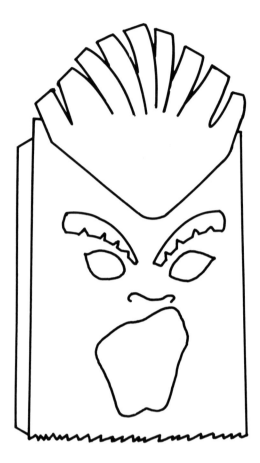

Fig. 4-7. A sack mask is a great project for Halloween.

Project 5

Make
Finger Paints

Age Group: 2 to 7

Time Required: 1 hour

Remember the squishy, messy activities of childhood? The soft mud squeezing out from between your toes as you deliberately walked barefoot after a big rain storm . . . the joy of rubbing your fingers through a messy, colorful paint mixture spread on big sheets of brown paper?

Parents usually frown on the messy activities that children love, fearing the childish chaos these activities cause. So, instead of your children surprising you with such a mess, why not plan the messy activity by making a special kind of "goo" for finger paintings? With your supervision and participation, the squishy material becomes a learning experience for your little ones.

Do you have a child who is adept at getting into things? This is the perfect project to show such a child that messy fun can be had with a parent's supervision. Let the child do as much measuring and mixing as possible. The child will learn to trust his or her own skills and both of you will enjoy a fun time filled with laughter.

When the paint is ready, create a safe workplace where newspapers or a painter's dropcloth covers a table and any other areas where paint might spill or splash. Let the children use their hands to spread the paints and make mixtures of different colors. You will have the opportunity to show them about different color mixtures.

A fun project like this one lets children be children. Be sensitive to your child's moods and notice when a child might be looking longingly out a window or sitting quietly on the sofa or a bed. You can bring excitement to a child when you declare: "Let's make a mess together."

Materials and Tools

◊ Finger paint recipe:
  • 1 envelop unflavored gelatin
  • $3/4$ cup cornstarch

- 2 cups hot water
- 1 teaspoon food coloring
- 1 teaspoon vinegar
- 1 cup cold water
- 3/4 cup liquid detergent
◊ Small mixing bowl
◊ Spoon
◊ Medium-sized pan
◊ Heavy paper
◊ Paper weights, such as food cans or tightly sealed jars
◊ Old shirts and pants
◊ Old newspaper
◊ Your stove

Getting Started

Try to surprise the children with this project. Before you announce that you have something special for them to do, put on your old clothes and make a grand entrance into the area where the children are playing or watching television. Tell them that you are going to help them have some messy fun. Then, help the children get ready for this project. Do you feel the excitement?

Choose your work area and encourage the children to help you prepare it. Show them how to spread old newspapers over the work surface. Putting newspapers on the floor is a good idea. When the work area is covered with a layer of newspapers, begin collecting your materials and tools.

Do the children want to make just one color or several different colors? If you have the time to make several different colored mixtures, consider teaching the children about blending colors and making different shades. This additional part of the project is discussed at the end of these instructions.

Mixing the Recipe

For each finger paint color you wish to make, mix the unflavored gelatin in 1/4 cup of cold water. One of the children can gently stir the mixture until all of the gelatin has dissolved in the water.

Mix the cornstarch and 3/4 cup of cold water in the pan. Put this mixture on the stove and heat it over medium heat. Add the hot water, stirring the mixture constantly until it boils.

STOP Are your children mature enough to help you around the stove? If so, let them add the hot water and stir—under your close supervision, of course.

Watch the pan on the stove. Do not let the cornstarch mixture boil over or dry out. When the cornstarch mixture begins boiling, make sure it is smooth and creamy. Then, stop stirring and remove the mixture from the heat. Slowly blend in the gelatin mixture as shown in Fig. 5-1.

Fig. 5-1. Mixing up finger paints.

Now, add the liquid detergent as you continue to stir the hot mixture of cornstarch and gelatin. Stir until the detergent has dissolved. At this point, the mixture should be a creamy, white color.

Ask your children to name their favorite color. Then, select the matching food coloring and blend one teaspoon of food coloring into one teaspoon of vinegar in a cup. Add the food color and vinegar mixture to the cornstarch and gelatin.

Allow the mixture to cool in the pan. Be sure the pan is sitting in a safe place so it will not be spilled or bumped.

While the mixture is cooling, place a heavy piece of paper on the work table for each child who will be painting.

Painting

When the mixture is cool to the touch, the children can begin using it. Allow each child to scoop out a goopy, drippy handful from the pan and plop it down on the heavy paper. You can enjoy their fun or you can begin your own finger painting.

Encourage each child to create a unique, yet simple, design. Fingers work so well for drawing long lines and for making circles. Show a child how to put a distinctive thumbprint somewhere in a picture. Hand prints are also wonderful in these paintings. I treasure the tiny hand prints I have collected over the years.

Don't be afraid of the mess. That's part of the fun. And when it is clean-up time you can encourage the children to share the chores.

When the children are finished with their paintings, set them aside to dry. Put a weight on each of the four corners of each sheet of paper to prevent curling as shown in Fig. 5-2.

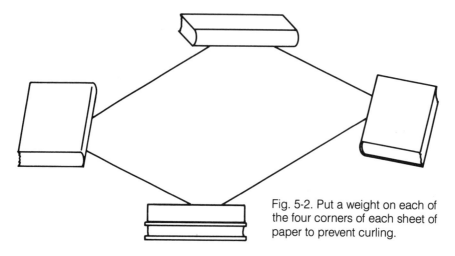

Fig. 5-2. Put a weight on each of the four corners of each sheet of paper to prevent curling.

Heavy cans of food work well to hold the corners of paint-soaked paper. Clean blocks of wood or small bricks also can be used.

Let the children proudly present their paintings to you. Children love to describe the colors and shapes just like Skippy is doing in Fig. 5-3.

Learning about Color

Make this project into a learning opportunity for the children. If you make several different colored mixtures, you can show the children about color and its various blends and shades.

Also, make a sample of the mixture without any food coloring in it. You can use it for shading the other colors.

Refer to an encyclopedia for detailed descriptions of colors. Then, try some of these simple color blends:

◇ Red blended with yellow makes a bright orange.
◇ Blue blended with yellow makes a slimy green.
◇ Red blended with blue makes a deep violet.

After making these simple color changes, try adding more of the original mixture to each color to lighten the original colors. Soon, you and the children will be enjoying an entire rainbow of bright and inviting

Fig. 5-3. Skippy describes his finger paintings to his dad.

colors that you have made with them. Because you shared in the fun perhaps you recalled the joys of your childhood. Keep your finger painting as a memory of this special time of old memories and new ones.

Remember, the children will think that clean-up time is fun, too, if you encourage them to share the chores.

Make A
Falling Rain Picture

Age Group: 2 to 7
Time Required: 2 hours

Have you ever visited an art gallery with your children and had them discover a picture they thought looked very real? Many times, my own children have seen beautiful and realistic pictures and then worked very hard for a long time trying to make their works of art look just as real. Usually, each child would eventually become discouraged and quit, feeling frustrated with the results.

I would try to comfort them, but a mother's love can only do so much to comfort a child when the child's desires to achieve something exceeds his coordination and experience. Soon, I learned that a creative project that is properly suited for a child's ability will build confidence and encourage future creative endeavors. Now, I look forward to the time when a child says: "I want to paint a picture." I say: "Let's do a falling rain picture."

When your children express a desire to be creative, you can give them a project that is sure to delight them and encourage them. And, you can do a falling rain picture even on a sunny day.

A falling rain picture is a three-dimensional picture of a scene as it might look when the rain is falling. The project process causes the picture to look wet and drizzly. It is fun to make and, at the same time, this project gives your children practice on preschool activities such as gluing, cutting, painting, and coloring.

An even more important result of this project is the boost your child's self-esteem will receive. In a few short hours, your child will create a realistic picture that can be proudly displayed in the classroom, living room, office, or bedroom. Rather than a discouraging experience, your child will have a positive, successful experience with painting.

Materials and Tools

◇ Blunt scissors
◇ Ruler
◇ Glue
◇ Tracing paper
◇ Blue marker filled with water-soluble, nonpermanent color
◇ 1 sheet of blue construction paper
◇ 1 sheet of white construction paper
◇ Pencil
◇ Blue food coloring
◇ Spray bottle filled with water
◇ Plastic tablecloth or newspaper

Getting Started

Gather your materials and tools. Find a brightly lit place to work. The best work area for this project is on a table. Always protect the table you are using. Show the children how to cover the table with a plastic tablecloth or other protective covering such as a layer of old newspapers. After the children have covered the table, compliment them for doing a good job.

Have each child take a sheet of white construction paper and measure and mark a 1-inch-wide border along each side of the white paper as shown in Fig. 6-1. Encourage the children to draw dark, solid lines for this border. Now, have them cut along those lines to remove the 1-inch border.

Now, each child should draw the same 1-inch border on a sheet of blue construction paper. Do not cut the blue paper, but rather tell the children to glue their white piece directly in the center of the blue piece of construction paper. The children will be delighted when they see that the blue piece of construction paper forms a frame around the white paper.

Transferring the Patterns

Transfer the pattern of the duck and his bill from Fig. 6-2 to pieces of colored construction paper. What colors are a duck and his bill? Use yellow construction paper for the duck's body and use orange construction paper for the bill. Then, transfer the pattern for the water from Fig. 6-3 to blue construction paper.

You can do this in one of two ways. You can cut the duck and the water directly from the page of this book using the scissors. On the other hand, to preserve the book, you might wish to have the children trace the duck and the water on tracing paper.

To trace the patterns, show the children how to use the tracing paper. Have the children place the thin tracing paper over the figure to be transferred. While you steady the tracing paper, encourage each child

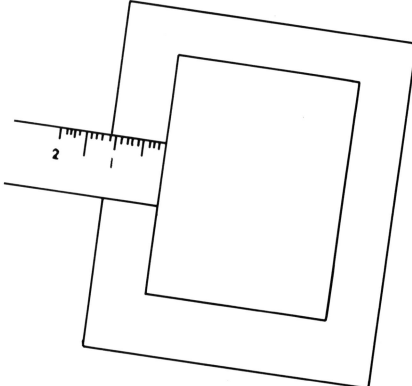

Fig. 6-1. Measure in 1 inch from each side.

to follow the lines in the figure with a pencil. Take the sheet of tracing paper from the page in the book and cut out the pattern for the duck and for the water. Tape or glue the tracing paper to the sheets of colored construction paper and cut around the tracing paper.

Putting the Picture Together

First, put together the parts cut out from the patterns. Glue the duck's bill to the duck's body.

Now, glue the water onto the bottom of the white background of your picture.

The falling rain picture will be three dimensional. To make a picture appear three dimensional, certain parts of it will have to stand out away from the background. In this picture, the duck will stand out. Tell the children to measure the body of the duck that they cut out. Then, measure and cut a piece of white construction paper 1 inch wide that will fit on the back of the duck. Fold the section of paper in half along the length of the paper.

Glue one side of the folded paper to the back of the body of the duck. Then, put a little glue on the other side of the folded piece of paper

Fig. 6-2. Pattern for duck and bill.

Fig. 6-3. Pattern for water.

on the back of the duck's body as shown in Fig. 6-4. Turn the duck over and press the small gluey section onto the water. This gives the duck a three-dimensional effect because it stands out from the water. Already, at this point, the children have created a neat picture. Be sure to give compliments to all.

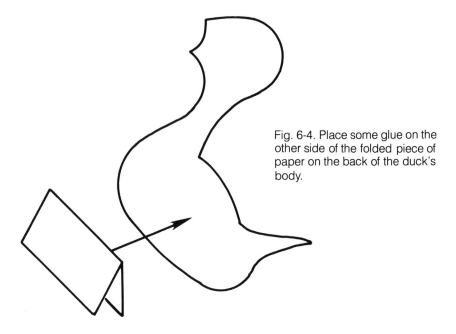

Fig. 6-4. Place some glue on the other side of the folded piece of paper on the back of the duck's body.

Creating Rain

Are you ready for a rain shower? Show the children how to use the blue, water-soluble marker to make blue spots like rain drops all over the picture of the duck on the water.

Hold up the spotted picture and begin spraying it. Turn the spray bottle nozzle so it sprays a fine mist and "spritz" the picture. Start at the top of the picture and work back and forth across the picture until all the blue spots are wet and runny. The water-soluble blue color will run in streaks down the picture creating the realistic impression of blurry raindrops, just as on a rainy day.

Lay the picture flat again and allow the streaks of rain to dry. When the water-soluble blue color is dry, the picture is ready to be displayed.

Your children will be thrilled about the realistic picture they have made. Hang it up or enter it in a children's art contest. Your pride in your children's work will make the children want to succeed. In a few short hours, you have helped your children take a big step towards self-confidence and future achievements.

Making a falling rain picture gives you the opportunity to praise your children for their creative efforts. Each child will be able to see something special come from his own creative work. And you will have a picture that you and your children can display with pride.

Project 7

Make A Toy Parachute

Age Group: 2 to 7
Time Required: 10 minutes

One warm, sunny day, when my boys were small, they all came as one, bursting into the kitchen, to tell me about a new toy that they had seen at another child's house. A toy company had introduced model army men with accompanying planes and parachutes. My three boys, all talking at the same time, explained that they were not so much interested in the airplanes and men as they were interested in the graceful, floating parachutes.

Outside, they had watched their friend carefully fold the parachute around the army man and then toss the plastic figure into the sky. High in the sky, the parachute unfolded and the figure danced and floated down in the breeze. The delighted child ran and caught the parachute man in his hand. Seeing such fun had sent my own children running for home to beg for this neat toy.

Each toy parachute man was expensive and I had to multiply the proposed purchase by three. I needed only one moment to realize that I could not run right to the store and make such a purchase.

It was difficult to look at the expectant faces of my three boys. Then I realized that we could make our own parachutes and attach them to any number of the many toy soldiers, astronauts, race car drivers, firemen, cowboys, and other characters already cluttering up shelves and boxes in the boys' bedrooms and playroom. So, mustering my most enthusiastic voice, I informed my three expectant little ones that we would make our own parachute men.

Are you looking for a simple activity that does not require much thought or time? If you are busy today, you might have very little free time to spend with your children. This quick project allows you to enjoy yourselves doing something together.

Make one or several toy parachutes with your children and then spend your remaining time watching the children play with the parachutes. You will see their eyes shine as the parachutes float softly through the air.

This project takes about ten minutes to complete but the finished parachute provides hours of playtime. Making and using the parachute teaches coordination in little hands and the children will delight in chasing and catching the parachutes as they float to the ground.

Why not make a parachute together today?

Materials and Tools

◇ 1 plastic bag or sheet of lightweight plastic
◇ 1 toy soldier, astronaut, or other character
◇ 1 spool of heavy thread or fishing line
◇ Transparent tape
◇ Marker or crayon that will mark on plastic
◇ Scissors
◇ Ruler

Getting Started

Gather your materials. Any type of plastic sack will work fine for this project. It could be clear, white, yellow, black, or green. However, you must be able to cut an eight-inch square from the plastic for every parachute you wish to make. When searching for a plastic bag or scrap plastic sheets, keep a ruler handy to measure the plastic.

While you are searching for the plastic bag, send each child off to find the favorite toy figure that will become the parachute man. Regroup at the kitchen table or, if it is a nice day, at a patio or deck table. Being outside only heightens the excitement surrounding such a project.

Show each child how to use a ruler to measure an eight-inch square on the piece of plastic. Use a marker or crayon to draw heavy, dark lines to form the square on the plastic.

Encourage each child to cut the plastic. However, plastic is very difficult to cut with scissors. Be prepared to offer a word of praise when tiny hands grow tired. Then, finish the cutting job, if necessary.

From the roll of thread or fishing line, measure and cut two pieces of line, each 16 inches long.

Spread out the piece of plastic. Show the children each corner of the piece and explain that the two pieces of line will be attached to opposite corners of the square piece of plastic.

There are two ways to attach the lines to the plastic. One way is to use small pieces of transparent tape to hold the lines. With small pieces of tape, secure one end of each piece of line to an opposite corner so that the two pieces of line cross each other over the middle of the square piece of plastic. Be sure that the line is securely covered by the tape.

Another way to join the lines to the plastic is to simply tie the end of each line to the corner of the square of plastic. You will probably have to do this step because little ones are easily frustrated by any step that requires tying.

Does your parachute look like the one in Fig. 7-1?

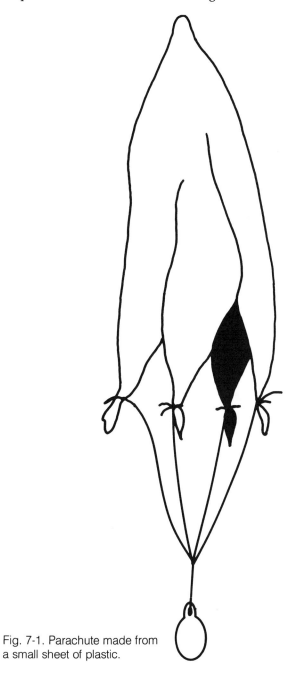

Fig. 7-1. Parachute made from a small sheet of plastic.

Pick up the parachute by the lines and let it hang from your fingers. Be sure that the lines are even. Gather the lines together in the center near where they cross over your fingers. Using another short piece of thread or fishing line, tie the lines together with a simple knot. Leave enough line to go around the figure that will be your parachute man. Tie the threads around the toy figure. If no toy figure "volunteers" for the parachute ride, you might substitute a lead fishing weight or a heavy metal nut such as a lug nut from a car or truck.

Folding the Parachute

Is everyone ready to go outside and toss the parachutes? Take a moment to show the children a simple folding technique that will help the parachute go higher and work better.

Lay the plastic square on the table and fold it so the four corners are together as in Fig. 7-2. Fold up corners one and two as in Fig. 7-3, and again as in Fig. 7-4. Then, roll up the parachute beginning at the top and rolling toward the weight. Wrap the threads loosely around the outside of the parachute but be careful to not tangle the threads.

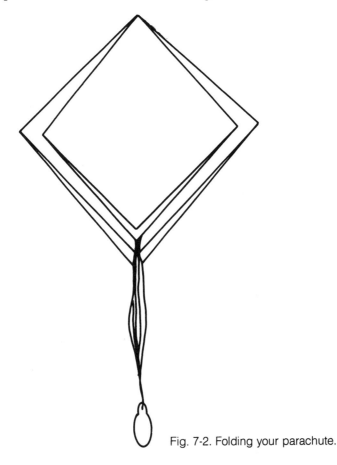

Fig. 7-2. Folding your parachute.

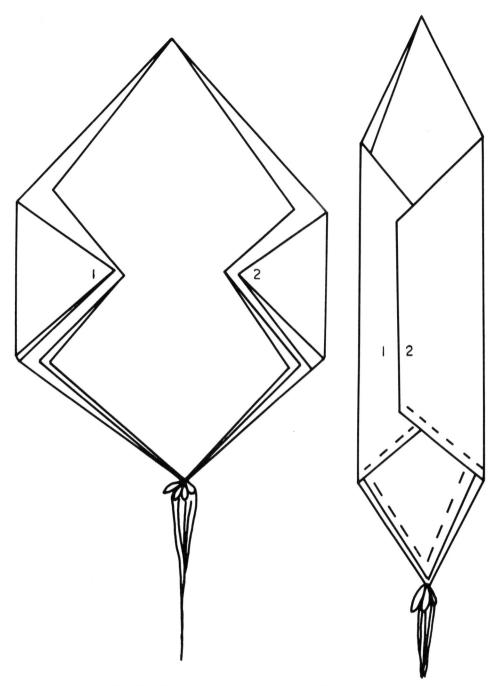

Fig. 7-3. Fold the corners in . . .

Fig. 7-4. . . . then fold them in again.

This folding technique is not necessary but does help the parachute propel itself higher when it is thrown. If your children would rather throw their parachutes from a high place, such as off a balcony or a high deck, the folding technique is not necessary.

Remember to check your children's outdoor play area for any low power lines. Tell your children to stay away from power lines wherever they play. Also, watch out for trees that might snag a parachute. Children are often tempted to climb into danger to recover a toy.

Throwing, chasing, and catching a parachute man will provide a child with hours of healthy, outdoor fun. While you might not be able to spend those hours with your child, you will have helped with the most important part of the project—making the parachute.

My three boys all enjoyed the parachutes we made together on that afternoon so long ago.

Project 8

Make A
Flower Greeting Card
And Envelope

Age Group: 2 to 7

Time Required: 2 hours. If fresh flowers are used in this project, they must be pressed and dried for at least 3 days before use.

Everyone loves to know that someone cares about him enough to make something special just for him. A handmade greeting card is a wonderful way to make someone feel good. Handmade cards say exactly what you want them to say, saving you a long search for just the right one. With a handmade card, a trip to the grocery store or card shop in the mall is not necessary.

Grandparents, aunts, uncles, parents, and friends know you care when they receive these cards. They know you and the children spent time making these cards especially for them. Think of the joy that an elderly person will feel when one of these cards arrives in the mail. The day of someone who is hospitalized will be much brighter when the nurse delivers your child's card.

A handmade card also is a way to teach children to say "thank you" for Christmas and birthday gifts, overnight visits at friends' homes, and for other special favors. Teaching children to share and say "thank you" is a challenge, but in our family, I have found my children respond more favorably when learning is fun.

When a child is thinking about a relative who lives hundreds or thousands of miles away, you can suggest a handmade card as a way to just say hello. There are many occasions to send a handmade card. Just try this project together and enjoy the results.

Materials and Tools

◊ Construction paper
◊ Typing paper
◊ Transparent tape
◊ Old newspaper
◊ Several heavy books, such as encyclopedias
◊ Pressed wild flowers or silk flowers
◊ Glue
◊ Blunt scissors
◊ Color markers
◊ Clear plastic contact paper
◊ Pencils
◊ Large white or brown envelopes

Gathering Flowers

The front of each card will be covered with beautiful flowers to create an attractive, three-dimensional effect. Do you have a flower garden that might supply some daisies or a delicate rose? Wildflowers that you and your children might find growing in your yard, in a vacant field, or along a country road also would be perfect for a card. If flowers are not in season, you can purchase lovely silk flowers from a discount store or craft shop. If you and your children want real flowers out of season, you can buy them from any florist.

My family lives in Iowa where wild flowers are abundant in the spring, so finding the beautiful field flowers for the card is a rewarding experience in itself. If you can go into the country when flowers are blooming, you can have a similar experience. Go to the public library and find a book on the different wild flowers in your region. Take the wildflower book along on your search and this project could be a wonderful way for you and your children to learn more about your region of the country.

Let each child select the flowers for the card to be made. Be sure that each flower has a nice, long stem and firm, fresh petals.

Pressing and Drying the Flowers

If you use fresh flowers, you must first press and dry them. Fresh flowers are full of moisture that will cause mildew under the clear contact paper you will use to cover the flowers.

To press and dry your fresh flowers, carefully place each flower between two layers of newspaper as shown in Fig. 8-1. Spread out the petals so they will be visible after the flower has been pressed. Place each flower under a stack of heavy books. The weight of the books will flatten the flower and squeeze out the natural moisture that will soak into the newspapers. Allow the flowers to dry for at least three days under the stack of books.

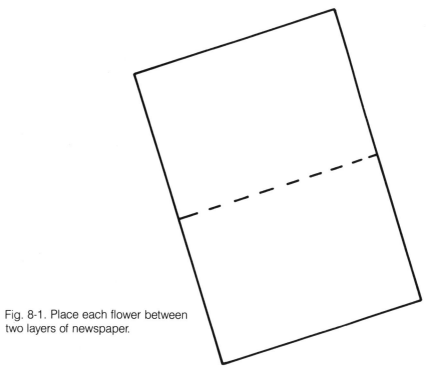

Fig. 8-1. Place each flower between two layers of newspaper.

Making the Card

Gather your other materials. Clear contact paper is most often used to cover shelves in kitchen cabinets. If you do not have clear contact paper, you will find rolls of it at your grocery store or discount center. Find a brightly lit workplace. A table in the kitchen is a good work surface. Although you and the children are not painting in this project, it is always a good idea to cover the table you are using with old newspapers or some other type of pad or cloth.

Taking time to properly prepare for a project teaches children to do things correctly and in order.

If more than one child is doing this project with you, have the children pair off. It is time to pick the construction paper to be used in each card. Each card will actually be made from half of the sheet of construction paper.

When the children have chosen a color, have them lay out the piece of the colored construction paper flat on the table. Do this for every card that the children are going to make.

Show the children how to fold each piece of construction paper in half and crease the fold so that the paper is easier to cut, as shown in Fig. 8-2. Ask each pair of children to decide who will cut the paper in half. Have the children take the scissors and cut along the crease as shown in Fig. 8-3. When the children are finished, explain to them how they suc-

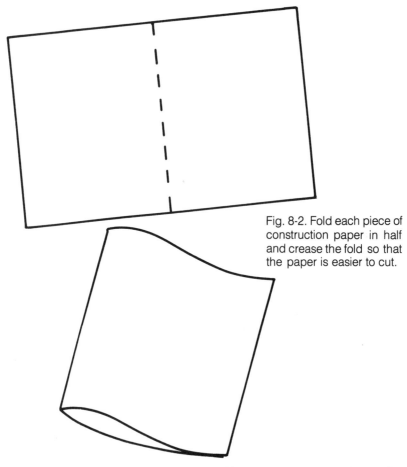

Fig. 8-2. Fold each piece of construction paper in half and crease the fold so that the paper is easier to cut.

ceeded in cutting the paper exactly in half without using a ruler and a pencil to measure and mark the paper. They have all done something special.

Now, each child has a piece of construction paper. Have the children fold the piece of paper in half. Then, let the children decide which side they want to be the front of each greeting card. Now they are ready for their flowers.

Suggest several ways to arrange the flowers on the card. Your children might want to draw a vase on some colored construction paper, cut it out, and glue it on the card for the flowers to be arranged in as shown in Fig. 8-4. Use your imagination and create your own design. Your children will learn from you and come up with their own creative ideas.

Now, it's time to glue the flowers to the front of the construction paper card. Show the children how to apply a small line of glue to the stem of each flower, gently bending the petals so that they spread out over the construction paper. Set the card aside for about five minutes so that the glue can begin drying.

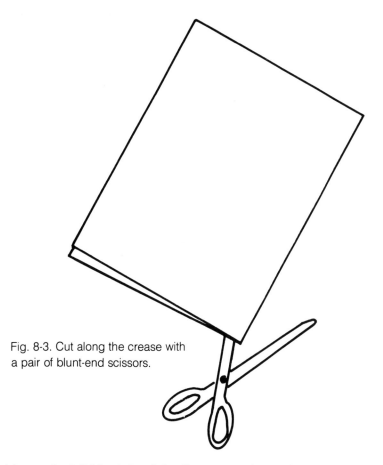

Fig. 8-3. Cut along the crease with
a pair of blunt-end scissors.

After each child has glued the flowers on the card, encourage them
to write a message, in pencil, on the front of the card. The message
should give the reader a clue about what kind of card they are receiving.
This message could be written anywhere around the flowers on the front
of the card. Be prepared to help spell words such as "happy," "birthday,"
"grandma," and "teacher." Encourage little ones who are easily frustrated by spelling errors and frequent erasing. The cards will still be
beautiful.

After each child is happy with the message on the front of the card,
have them cover the pencil lines with colored markers or crayons for a
bright, bold card.

Finishing the Card

Now, you are ready to help the children preserve their flowers and
cards by covering the front of each card with clear contact paper. This is a
step you will have to do because the children might find it too difficult. Because contact paper is sticky, you should handle it as shown in
Fig. 8-5.

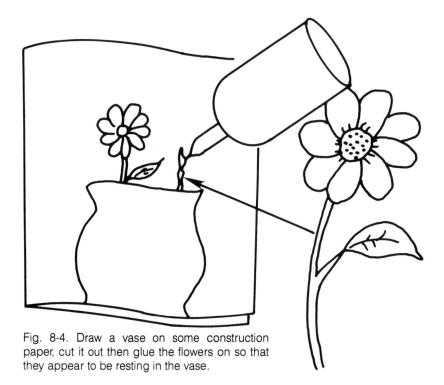

Fig. 8-4. Draw a vase on some construction paper, cut it out then glue the flowers on so that they appear to be resting in the vase.

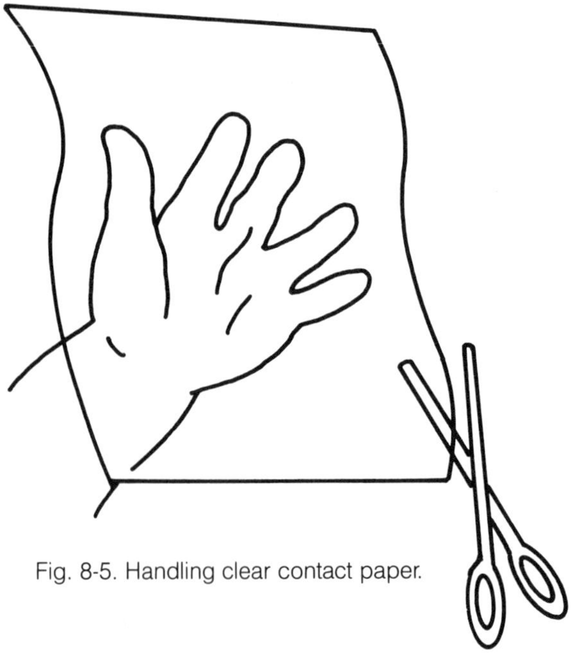

Fig. 8-5. Handling clear contact paper.

Roll out just enough of the paper to make a rectangular shape that is slightly larger than the size of the card. Leave an edge of clear contact paper big enough to overlap all four sides of the card.

Remove the protection paper from the back of the rectangular sheet of clear contact paper and center it above the front of the card. Lay it carefully onto the top of the card and press firmly. Once the rectangle of contact paper is in place, let eager, little hands help press the contact paper over the flowers.

To prevent bubbles from forming under the contact paper where it touches the flat surface of the construction paper, roll the contact paper with a pencil to drive out any trapped air.

You will have to turn the overlapping edges of the contact paper over the edges of the construction paper and press firmly. Now, a beautiful flower is preserved for someone else to share.

Your child can now turn to the inside of the card. This is the place for each child's personal expression of love to the individual who will receive the card. Before the children begin writing their special messages, gather pictures of the persons who will receive these cards. Place the pictures in the middle of your work area so that the children can see the loved ones they are writing to.

Fig. 8-6. The completed flower greeting card.

Do your finished cards look like the one that Skippy made as shown in Fig. 8-6? When each card is finished, you can supply the right size of envelope, or the children can make an envelope from a sheet of white typing paper. Take a sheet of white typing paper and fold it in half. Help the children use the transparent tape to seal two sides of the folded paper, leaving an open top for the card to slip through. Let each child place the card in the envelope and then seal the top of it with another strip of transparent tape.

Show the children how important these cards are to you by immediately addressing them. Whisk the children off to the car and drive them and their cards down to the local post office for proper postage. Then, let each child drop his card into the mail slot. Happiness is now on its way to a loved one.

The card in the mail is now a personal expression of your children's love or friendship. No one else will receive a card quite like it.

Make A
Model Rocket Shop

Age Group: 3 to 10

Time Required: 2 hours

It seems that boys are born with the desire to build plastic model kits. It must have something to do with their chromosomes. With three creative boys in my family, model cars, trucks, airplanes, and anything else that was fun to assemble were always in demand.

If I would even think of trying to buy a model kit for a birthday or for Christmas, I would shudder because of the possibility of buying something that the boys had already put together. Even worse was the possibility that I might buy one that was "dumb" or represented an out-of-date car or plane.

Do your children enjoy putting together models? Maybe you have found the cost of some of the models you wanted to buy prohibitive. Imagine being able to assemble a model anytime the mood hit because the materials are right at your finger tips.

The model rocket ship in this project is easy to assemble and inexpensive. It is made from toilet paper rolls or paper towel rolls, straws, and paper cups. When these simple items are put together correctly, they form a single- or multiple-stage rocket ship. Give this project a try and just see if you and your children are not delighted with the results.

Materials and Tools

◇ Cardboard toilet paper tube
◇ Cardboard paper towel tube
◇ Heavy typing paper, not the erasable type
◇ White construction paper or lightweight cardboard
◇ Drinking straws
◇ Model airplane glue
◇ Tempera paint
◇ Cutting tool
◇ Scissors

Gathering Your Materials and Getting Started

Gather your materials and tools and find a brightly lit workplace suited to cutting and gluing. A table where you and your children can sit and work is preferable.

You can accumulate various tubes from empty rolls of toilet paper or paper towel rolls if you plan ahead to do this activity. You can buy white drinking straws, tempera paint, model airplane glue, and white construction paper from a grocery store or discount center.

Put on some old clothes so you will not get paint or glue on your good things. Begin the project by spreading newspaper over the table top to catch the splatters of paint or drips of glue.

This is an activity your children can do with minimal help.

Now that your work surface is prepared, place the toilet paper roll on the table in front of the children. Tell one child to trace the circle in Fig. 9-1 and then cut it out. Remember to trace and cut the line going from the edge of the circle to the middle of the circle. This cut allow the children to roll the circle into a cone shape until it fits the end of the toilet paper roll. The cone shape is the nose of the rocket. Have the children run a small line of glue along the top of the tube and place the cone on the roll.

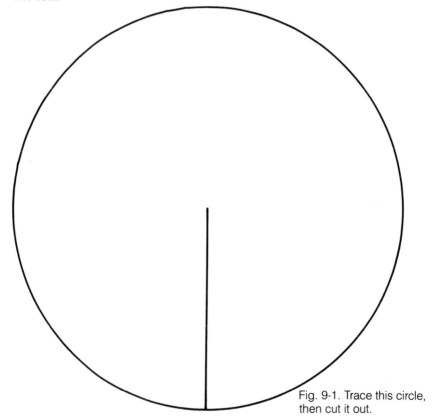

Fig. 9-1. Trace this circle, then cut it out.

Adding the Rocket's Fins

Figure 9-2 shows the fins of the rocket ship. Let the children choose the shape they want to use, then trace the fin four times and cut four fins. When the fins are traced and cut, you take the cutting tool and cut four small slits in the cone. Place a little glue on the side ends of the fins and slip each one separately into the slits as shown in Fig. 9-3. Now measure the length of the top of the fin and cut a straw to that measurement. Glue the section of straw onto the rocket ship on either side of the fin, as shown in Fig. 9-4. Put four short pieces of straw on the inside bottom of the tube as shown in Fig. 9-5. This represents the booster rockets that help the rocket leave the ground.

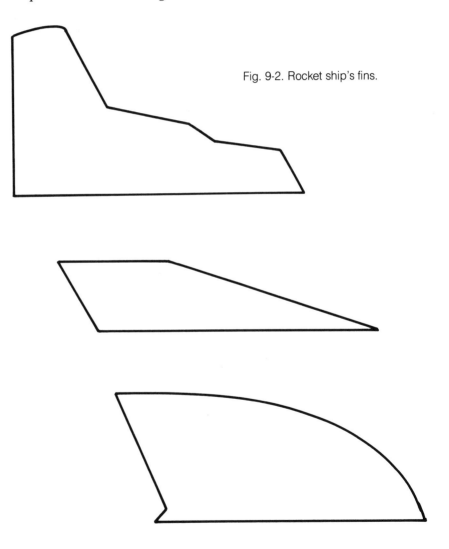

Fig. 9-2. Rocket ship's fins.

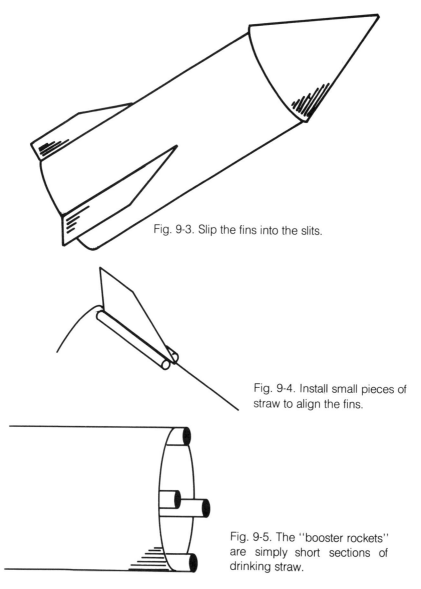

Fig. 9-3. Slip the fins into the slits.

Fig. 9-4. Install small pieces of straw to align the fins.

Fig. 9-5. The "booster rockets" are simply short sections of drinking straw.

If the children would like to make a multistage rocket ship, use a slightly larger paper towel tube. Glue the paper cone on it and slip it inside the bottom of the smaller rocket before the booster rocket straws are added. Trim the bottom edge of the cone so the edge is even with the tube after it is glued inside the other rocket section. Now, tell the children to follow the same directions as with the smaller rocket for gluing on the fins and sections of straws on either side of the fins. When the children have finished gluing the rocket ship together, tell them to decorate it with tempera paint. The single stage rocket might look something like the one shown in Fig. 9-6.

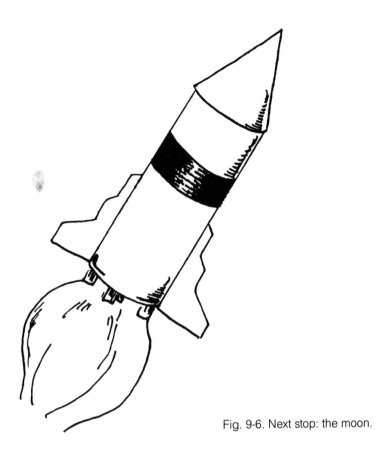

Fig. 9-6. Next stop: the moon.

Project 10

Make A Paper Airplane And Hat

Age Group: 2 to 7

Time Required: A few minutes for a simple paper airplane; or up to 1 hour for an elaborately decorated hat.

Do you remember making paper airplanes and hats when you were small? I spent a good portion of my childhood growing up with two older brothers and one younger brother. We often made paper airplanes for impromptu flying contests and the paper hats were wonderful for games of make believe.

I proudly wore my paper hat across my head while I pretended to be a nurse, sharply dressed all in white. On many occasions, paper hats served my brothers as "coonskin hats" in games of "Davy Crockett and the Indians."

Each time we would make hats or airplanes, there was excitement in the air. The hats never looked the same and the airplanes never seemed to fly the same. There was no explanation for the change but the suspense of seeing how each would turn out caused us to make one try after another.

Paper airplanes and hats only require a few pieces of paper and a little practice. Even sheets of newspaper or the brown paper from grocery sacks can serve as the raw materials for hats and planes. Crayons and colored markers can be used to make bold designs on the paper before or after folding. Just follow the directions and enjoy the activity together. When your children become adept at folding these shapes they will be able to make these toys on their own.

With this project, you will teach your children to use their skills and imaginations to make something that is fun to play with. Then they will be able to entertain themselves.

Materials and Tools

◇ Several sheets of paper:
  • Typing paper

- Notebook paper
- Old newspapers
- Paper sacks
◊ Crayons or markers
◊ Glue
◊ Glitter, stickers, and other decorations
◊ Vast quantities of imagination

Planning a Design for a Hat

Do your children have a favorite character from a Bible story, television show, or book? Does this favorite character wear a hat, helmet, crown, or headdress?

Encourage your children's imaginations. Lay a single sheet of paper flat on a tabletop, the floor, or other work area. Show the children how to fold the paper in the middle as shown in Fig. 10-1. Fold the corners to meet the center of the paper, as in Fig. 10-2. Encourage your children to read these directions and do as much of the folding as they can. This activity helps them learn to follow written directions.

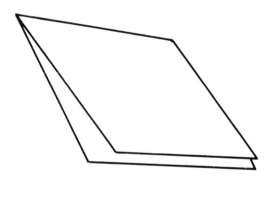

Fig. 10-1. Begin by folding the paper in the middle.

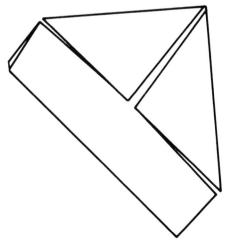

Fig. 10-2. Fold the corners to meet at the center of the paper.

Younger children will need much more help and encouragement than older children so be ready with a loving word and a helping hand. Children aged six or seven will learn the folding techniques quickly, and might find help unnecessary the second time they fold the paper hat.

Next fold the bottom flap up and bend the corners over as shown in Fig. 10-3. The folded side should look like the last illustration step shown in Fig. 10-3.

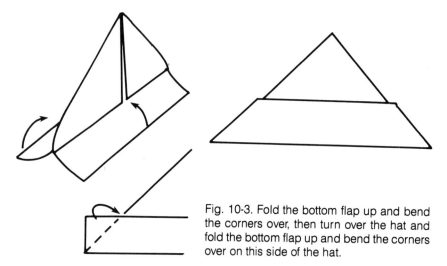

Fig. 10-3. Fold the bottom flap up and bend the corners over, then turn over the hat and fold the bottom flap up and bend the corners over on this side of the hat.

Turn over the hat and fold that bottom flap up and bend the corners over on this side of the hat. If the children do not yet understand how to do this, refer again to Fig. 10-3.

Open the hat in the middle and push the points together at the bottom as shown in Fig. 10-4.

Fold up points A and B so they meet. Please refer to Fig. 10-5. Do the same on both sides of the hat.

Finishing a Hat

The finished product will look like Fig. 10-6. Now, the children can have fun adding colors, designs, and decorations to the hat. Will it be a fairy's crown, the magic helmet of a mighty warrior, or part of some other costume like the one Skippy is wearing in Fig. 10-7?

When the children have finished decorating, have them put on their hats and look in a mirror so they can admire their creations. Be sure and praise each and every hat. The children will want to fold the hat shapes again and again.

Choosing the ''Right'' Paper for an Airplane

Notebook paper torn from a spiral-bound notebook or taken from a package of paper for three-ring binders is an excellent shape and size for

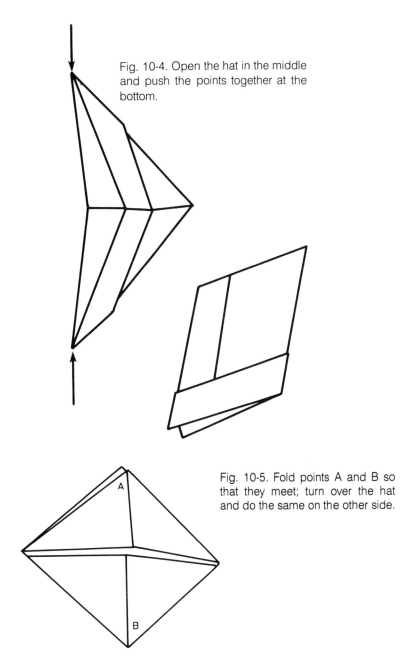

Fig. 10-4. Open the hat in the middle and push the points together at the bottom.

Fig. 10-5. Fold points A and B so that they meet; turn over the hat and do the same on the other side.

use in folding paper airplanes. Begin your folding technique in the same manner as with the paper hats. Fold one sheet the length of the notebook paper as shown in Fig. 10-8.

Reopen the sheet as in Fig. 10-9. Using the center fold line as a guide, show the children how to fold the tips toward that center fold line.

Fig. 10-6. The completed paper hat.

Fig. 10-7. General Skippy is ready to command his troops.

Note the dotted lines in Fig. 10-10. These lines show the folding procedures you have already done. The solid lines are the final folds and represent the paper airplane that has been completed to now.

Fold the paper airplane in half again as shown in Fig. 10-11.

Fold the wing tip down so the wings stand out as shown in Fig. 10-12.

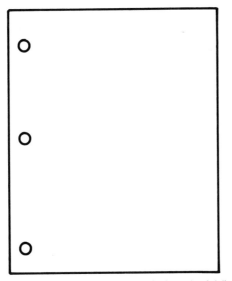

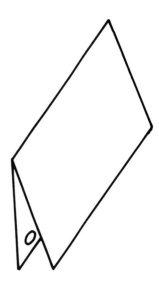

Fig. 10-8. Start your paper airplane by folding a piece of notebook paper in half.

Fig. 10-9. Reopen the folded paper and fold the top tips toward the center crease as shown.

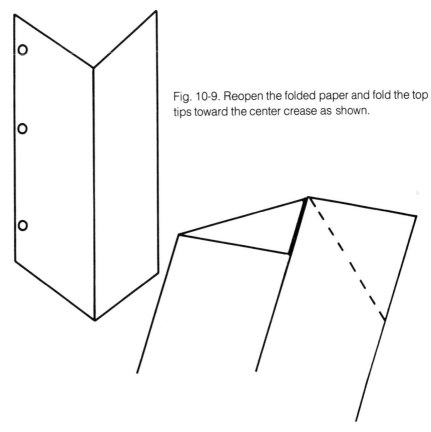

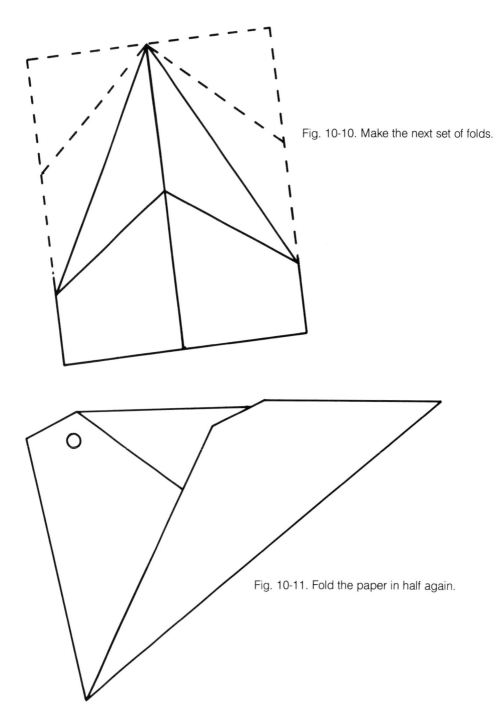

Fig. 10-10. Make the next set of folds.

Fig. 10-11. Fold the paper in half again.

Fig. 10-12. Fold the wing tip down.

Fig. 10-13. Captain Skippy of the Royal Air Force.

Now, put your airplane to the test and launch it into the air. Your children will enjoy tossing the airplane again and again as Skippy is doing in Fig. 10-13.

When you do this project with your children, you are giving them a valuable gift. You are teaching them to make simple toys that they can use to amuse themselves when they are alone or with friends. You are teaching them to use their imaginations and develop their hand–eye coordination.

While you are making paper hats and airplanes, be sure the television and radio are turned off. Help the children to concentrate on what they are doing. It will make the project more fun for everyone.

When the children have finished making paper hats, provide other articles of dress-up clothing that will make playtime exciting and fun. Perhaps you have something that might serve as a cape. An adult's old coat can be transformed by imagination into a soldier's uniform. Use your imagination.

Project 11

Make A
Winter Wonderland Jar

Age Group: 2 to 7
Time Required: 2 hours

When I was a child, we had on the shelf in our living room bookcase a lovely little clear glass globe on a pedestal. Inside the globe was a winter scene of a deer in a forest. When I picked up the globe and shook it, snow would flurry around the deer and the tree and fall lightly to the bottom of the globe. I was enchanted by the swirling flakes of snow and would shake the globe and then hold myself as still as I possibly could, watching the patterns made by the flakes as they fell over and around the deer and the tree inside the globe.

Heidi, in the story of her life in Switzerland, also treasured a small wintry globe that belonged to her grandfather. She took it with her when she was taken from her grandfather's home on the mountain and placed with her relatives in town. When she became homesick for the mountain, she would watch the snow in the globe and remember her life in the mountains with her grandfather.

You can make a winter wonderland jar similar to the one in the story about Heidi. Then, you too can enjoy a winter wonderland all year long. Your winter wonderland scene is just a simple baby food jar, a miniature plastic tree usually purchased for model train sets, a small plastic animal also from a hobby shop or toy store, and a few other simple items.

Materials and Tools
◇ Epoxy glue
◇ Empty baby food jar with lid
◇ Miniature spruce tree
◇ White aquarium sand rock
◇ Silver glitter
◇ Newspaper
◇ Plastic miniature animal

◇ Cuticle stick
◇ Rolls of cotton

Getting Started

Gather your materials and ask your children to lay old newspaper over your work surface. This will catch the extra drops of glue or glitter that might spill while you assemble the project. Discount stores that handle train sets will have the background scenery for a train table, such as trees, signs, and other things to make the setting for the train to travel through. Tell your children to choose a tiny tree and an animal for their winter wonderland jar. You will also find epoxy glue, cuticle sticks, white aquarium sand rock, and glitter at a discount store.

Have the children take the lid off of the jar and place it on the newspaper covered surface so the inside of the lid is exposed. Caution: Epoxy glue is dangerous to small children. Handle the glue yourself and keep it out of reach of your children. Read the back label containing directions on what to do in case of accidental contact with eyes or prolonged skin contact. Prevent accidents by using extreme caution.

Spread the glue evenly on the inside of the baby jar lid, then pour a fine layer of white aquarium sand rock into the glue base. While the glue is still sticky, place the miniature tree and animal into the glue base as shown in Fig. 11-1. Push the rock aside and make a small hole in the sand rock, pouring the epoxy into the hole, then place the tree into the glue base and push the sand rock up around the base of the tree with a cuticle stick. Do the same with the miniature animal. Avoid getting the epoxy on your fingers. Set the lid aside to dry for at least 45 minutes.

While the glue is drying, tell your children to fill the jar with water and sprinkle about 1/4 teaspoon of silver glitter into the water. When you are certain the glue is dry, have the children turn the lid, with the miniatures attached, over onto the top of the jar of water and tighten the lid.

Fig. 11-1. Beginning your winter wonderland jar.

GLUE

Sealing the Jar

Now, it is your turn to work with the glue again. Use the orange stick to spread epoxy around the lid opening. This will seal the lid tightly so water does not escape from the jar. Make a pretty base for the winter wonderland jar by applying glue with the cuticle stick around the edges of the lid and wrapping cotton around the lid. Cotton comes in long rolls and can be purchased at a discount or drug store. The long roll of cotton attached to the jar resembles snow drifts and adds a touch of charm to the winter scene.

Your winter wonderland jar is assembled. Does your jar look like the jar in Fig. 11-2? Shake the jar and watch the glitter drift over the miniature tree and animal. Winter wonder is with you all year round, just as it was with Heidi when she enjoyed her treasured snow globe from her grandfather.

Fig. 11-2. The completed winter wonderland jar.

Project 12

Make Baker's Clay Art

Age Group: 2 to 12

Time Required: 4 hours

On many a snowy afternoon, my children and I would work with what we called "our own Play Dough" at the dining room table. There are so many fascinating things to do with play dough, which is properly known as *baker's clay*.

Usually, we would begin our snowy or rainy afternoon by making our baker's clay. We made our own so we would have as much as we wanted.

Maybe you and your children enjoy play dough activities and would enjoy having some new ideas about how to make things with play dough. This activity suggests some art projects you and the children might find interesting enough to try. You can make almost any shape from play dough, allow it to dry and mount it or let it stand as a sculpture.

My children especially enjoyed making mounted wall plaques from our homemade play dough. Then, they would hang their plaques in their own rooms or give a plaque as a gift to relatives or friends.

Materials and Tools

◇ Recipe for baker's clay:
  • 4 cups flour
  • 1 cup salt
  • $1^1/_2$ cups water
◇ Bowl
◇ Spoon for stirring
◇ Piece of wood, such as paneling for walls
◇ Several colors of tempera or oil paints (red, green, yellow, and blue)
◇ Brushes

◇ Clear varnish
◇ Cleaning solution for brushes, such as turpentine
◇ Sharpened pencil
◇ Tracing paper
◇ Measuring cup
◇ Rolling pin
◇ Blunt kitchen knife
◇ Scissors
◇ Waxpaper
◇ Wood glue
◇ Cooking spray
◇ Cookie sheet
◇ Sandpaper
◇ Spatula

Getting Started

Gather your materials and tools and find a brightly lit, suitable work area. A table is the best work space for you and your children to sit together and work. Most of the materials for play dough art are found in your own kitchen cabinet. This is what makes making play dough so practical.

The only material you might have to buy is scrap paneling from a lumber yard or building center. You will need a 7-×-8-inch piece of scrap wall paneling for the car plaque and a 7-×-8-inch piece of wall paneling for a basket plaque.

Tempera paint is the easiest kind of paint to use because the brushes can be cleaned with water. Oil paint requires turpentine as a cleaning substance.

Making the Baker's Clay

Tell the children to mix the ingredients for baker's clay in a bowl just like Skippy is doing in Fig. 12-1. When the clay becomes stiff enough to shape, allow it to sit covered by a towel for a while.

Now would be a good time to go to a garage area or work shop and cut the wood for the plaques. Have the older children use a jig saw to cut the pieces of scrap paneling 7 × 8 inches. Use sandpaper to sand away the rough places around the edges of the plaque. Then, lay the pieces of wood aside on the table and begin again to work with the clay.

To make the car plaque, have the children trace the car shown in Fig. 12-2 and cut it out. Then, take a glob of baker's clay and lay it on a large piece of waxpaper. Use the rolling pin to roll out the dough into a flat mass similar to rolling out dough for a pie. Make it one-inch thick and just a bit bigger than your pattern of the car.

Tell the children to lay the pattern on the baker's clay and cut around it with a blunt kitchen knife. The waxpaper under the dough will prevent the dough from sticking to the surface of the table.

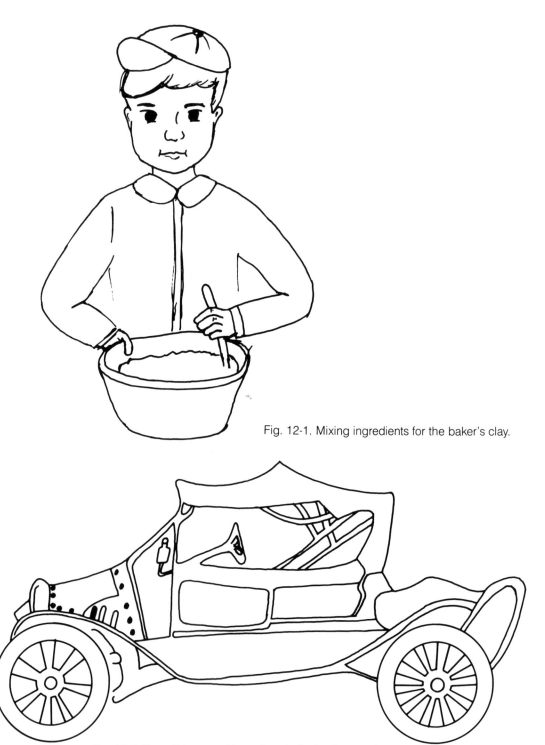

Fig. 12-1. Mixing ingredients for the baker's clay.

Fig. 12-2. Trace this car out to make a baker's clay car plaque.

With a sharpened pencil, draw the details on the car. You might have to do the drawing if your children do not feel they can copy the lines on the pattern. If they want to try drawing, they can easily rub out mistakes with their fingers. After the details are drawn, use a spatula to carefully lift the cut dough onto a cookie sheet that has been sprayed with a cooking spray. This keeps the dough from sticking to the surface of the cookie sheet.

Baking Your Dough Art

Turn on your oven to 200°F and place the dough art into the oven. Check the dough as it bakes and keep the heat low to prevent cracking. When the dough seems hard (about 5 minutes), remove the cookie sheet from the oven with pot holders and wait until it has cooled before continuing to work with it.

Prepare the paint and other tools while waiting to decorate the dough. When the dough is cool enough, have the children paint the car. Supervise the process and remind them that once a piece is painted, it cannot be changed, so they must be positive about their plan. When the car is painted wait about 25 minutes for the paint to dry.

Now have the children place glue on the plaque and press the car into the glue surface. Wood glue works the best. Have the children brush the surface of the plaque with clear varnish and set it aside to dry.

Follow the same procedure for forming the basket. Instead of drawing the design, the pieces are fit together like a puzzle. The basic pattern for the basket is shown on Fig. 12-3; the flowers, leaves, and other details are shown in Fig. 12-4. Have the children trace and cut out the base of the basket from Fig. 12-3 then trace and cut out all the flowers and leaves.

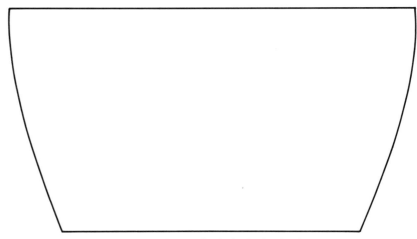

Fig. 12-3. Pattern for baker's clay basket.

Fig. 12-4. Pattern for flowers and leaves on the baker's clay basket.

Lay these pattern pieces on top of the dough and use the blunt kitchen knife to cut them from the dough.

Cut $1/2$-inch-wide strips as long as the width of the basket so the children can lay four strips across the width of the basket base and four on top of those so the basket appears to be woven. Along the top of the basket, twist another $1/2$-inch strip of dough and lay it over the woven flat strips.

Now, the children can lay the flowers and leaves on the top of the basket as though the flowers and leaves were arranged in the top of the basket. Skippy's finished basket is shown in Fig. 12-5 so you and the children can copy the arrangement he used.

Fig. 12-5. The completed baker's clay basket.

There are many other things you could do with play dough. Consider finding other picture ideas in magazines and using them as patterns. You and the children will want to make these and other play dough art objects again and again. Your younger children might want to just play with the dough. If so, place the play dough in a plastic bag, close it tight with a twist tie, and place it in the refrigerator.

Baker's clay play dough is stretchy, rolly fun. Your children will enjoy the play dough and the beautiful plaques they will make from it.

Project 13

Make A Shape Mobile

Age Group: 4 to 12
Time Required: 2 hours

Hanging up a mobile is a lively way to decorate any dull or uninteresting part of a room. Children and adults love brightly colored mobiles.

Mobiles come in all different forms. Mothers buy brightly colored mobiles to hang over a baby's crib to challenge a newborn's eyesight. Children enjoy wind mobiles that clatter in the wind. Teenagers buy mobiles to decorate their rooms, and adults enjoy fancy china mobiles found in novelty stores all over the county. Sailboats sail invisible waters, dolphins bound, gliders fly, and helicopters hover in many interesting mobiles.

Mobiles are popular because they are interesting to watch as they turn and move above the heads of the observer. The slightest draft sends the mobile gracefully moving on an unknown course.

This shape mobile is made of any shape you can imagine. And if you cannot think of a shape, the illustrations will provide you with a few ideas. The materials used are simple cardboard pieces cut into various shapes, brightly colored foil wrapping paper, and string.

Materials and Tools
◇ Scissors
◇ Cardboard
◇ Heavy-duty thread
◇ Colored foil
◇ Safety pin
◇ Glue
◇ Pointed tool, such as an ice pick or student's compass, to punch a hole
◇ Tracing paper
◇ Pencil

Gathering Your Materials

Gather your tools and materials and find a table in a brightly lit work area. The cardboard can be any corrugated box cut into sections for easier handling. Colored foil is found at craft stores. Discount centers sell colored foil during the Christmas season but do not do so during other periods of the year, unless some of the birthday wrapping paper is foil. Gold, green, red, and silver are the most common colors of foil, and some foil paper is even figured.

How to Make Your Shape Mobile

Ask the children to lay tracing paper on the pattern of the circle shown in Fig. 13-1. Then, have them cut the pattern from the tracing paper and lay it on the cardboard piece to transfer the circle. When the children have drawn around the circle, tell them to cut it out and lay it aside.

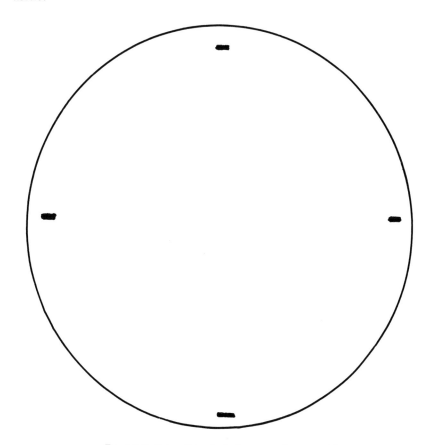

Fig. 13-1. Trace this circle for your shape mobile.

Use the circle pattern and transfer the shape to the color of foil the children have chosen. Make the foil circle slightly larger than the cardboard circle, and cut two foil circles so you are able to cover both sides of the cardboard circle. Next have the children glue the foil on both sides of the cardboard circle. Make sure the small overlapping edges are glued down securely. Have the children follow this same procedure with each of the hanging shapes they have chosen to trace from the shapes shown in Fig. 13-2.

Tell your children to unroll the thread and cut eight, two-foot lengths. Now, pick up the circle and use the pointed ice pick or compass to poke small holes in the suggested locations shown on the pattern piece shown in Fig. 13-1. Carefully make the holes yourself so the foil paper does not tear. Connect the lengths of thread onto the oval at the points shown in Fig. 13-1. Gather the threads together at one point above the shape and adjust them so the shape is balanced and hanging level. Twist them at the joining point and tie them onto the safety pin so the mobile can be hung.

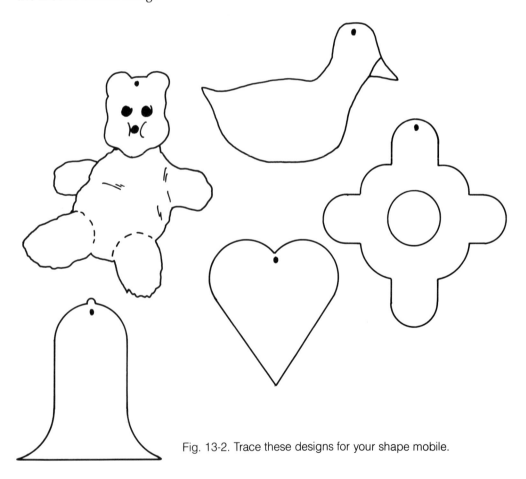

Fig. 13-2. Trace these designs for your shape mobile.

Have the children cut eight 2-foot lengths of heavy thread to be used to hang the other shapes you have made. Carefully punch two holes in the shapes that will hang on the top of the threads, and one hole on the top of the shape that will hang on the bottom of the string. Thread the first shape on the bottom, tying the thread in a knot so it will not slip through the hole. Carefully thread the second shape onto the thread through the two holes, tying a knot just before the first hole and just after the second hole. This way the shape will not slip down on the thread. Next, thread the top of the thread through one of the holes in the

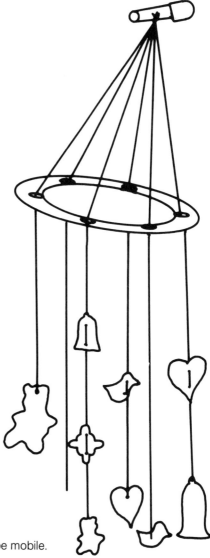

Fig. 13-3. The completed shape mobile.

circle and tie a knot in the top of the thread on the top side of the cardboard circle. Follow this procedure with each string of shapes. To prevent tearing of the foil, use small pieces of transparent tape on the holes after the threads are strung. Figure 13-3 shows a completed mobile.

Hang the mobile in your bedroom, playroom, or family room and enjoy the brightly colored foil shapes as they dazzle in the sunlight.

Project 14

Make A
Terrarium

Age Group: 2 to 12
Time Required: 2 hours

When I was about five, my parents took me to Colorado to see my grandmother. She lived in a little, main floor apartment in an older home where she kept a beautiful flower garden along the side of the house.

From then on, I often asked my mother and dad to plant flowers and, when I was old enough, I tried my hand at flower gardening. However, I was a failure with plants, so even though I worked hard to grow a garden, mine usually turned brown, or died from improper care.

How could I share something of my interest in growing things with my children? I was stymied until I discovered the terrarium. Do you love plants and flowers but just cannot seem to make them flourish as they should? Why not make a small terrarium? A *terrarium* is a garden under glass. The best thing about a terrarium is that it needs little care to flourish.

All you need to make a terrarium is a glass bowl, an old aquarium, or other glass container, and a lid or cover of some kind. Cactus, ferns, mosses, baby tears, small leaf begonias, or baby palms grow well in terrariums. Many small plants are perfect for this unique form of gardening.

Small terrariums make lovely table decorations inside the house. Children will be fascinated as they watch nature at work inside the container.

Materials and Tools
◇ Glass container
◇ Lid or top to cover the glass container
◇ Pair of tongs
◇ Fine gravel
◇ Activated charcoal

◇ Potting soil
◇ Plants
◇ Pebbles, small rocks, shells, interesting pieces of wood
◇ Spray bottle full of water
◇ Spoon for planting and moving the soil
◇ Fine sand
◇ Peat moss
◇ Newspaper

Gathering Your Materials and Tools

Purchase small, inexpensive palms, begonias, baby tears, mosses, ferns, or other similar plants. Take the children with you so they can choose their favorite plants.

The children also can carry the soil, fine gravel, activated charcoal, sand, and peat moss. Look around or call for the best prices. The plants will last for a long time and bring you and your family a lot of pleasure.

Choose a brightly lit work space on a table or cabinet where you and the children can work together. Spread newspaper over the work surface to catch the soil and other materials that might be spilled.

Place the glass container in front of your children. Tell the children to separate the soil, rocks, sand, peat moss, and fine gravel into various containers so that they are easily scooped into the spoon and placed into the glass container. Having your materials organized helps speed things along and makes assembling the terrarium more fun. Make sure all of your tools for assembling the terrarium are close by on the table. It's time to begin.

How to Assemble Your Terrarium

Have the children place about two inches of fine gravel along the bottom of the glass container. Help them spread it evenly all over the bottom of the container. Next, add a very thin layer of activated charcoal. Then, give the children another bowl and have them mix sterilized potting soil, sand, and peat moss together as you pour equal amounts of each into the bowl. Tell them to stir the mixture until all the materials are mixed well. They can spoon the mixture onto the top of activated charcoal. This is the final layer. The gravel, activated charcoal, and other mixtures in the soil help the water filter through the soil and keep it at the bottom in the gravel for the roots of the plants to absorb later.

Before the planting begins, draw the terrarium on a piece of paper and have the children plan how they want the plants arranged. Give them suggestions, but let the final plan be their own.

Give the spoon to the children and tell them to scoop out areas of the soil and put the small plants into the scooped-out areas. Help them make sure all the roots of each plant are covered well and use a little more soil to be sure they are. Have the children decorate the soil around the plants with the pretty pebbles, rocks, shells, and pieces of wood.

For the last step, use the spray bottle to moisten the soil and create a mist inside the terrarium. Cover the top of the glass container with a lid, or plastic wrap and a rubber band. Now, set the terrarium in a window so the plants will have light to help them grow. The light should be indirect sunlight.

Now, you have a beautiful terrarium just like the one shown in Fig. 14-1 to display on a table near a window to beautify your home. Your children will learn about growing plants and just what kind of care it takes to make them flourish. This form of gardening is easy and it will help your children understand nature and how they can help provide nourishment and care for these living things.

Fig. 14-1. Easy-to-make terrarium.

Project 15

Start A Crystal Garden

Age Group: 2 to 7

Time Required: 1 hour to prepare the crystal garden. Two days are required for the garden to grow.

Would you like to teach your children to enjoy science? One of the most fascinating areas of science is the chemistry of nature. A simple crystal garden can introduce the world of science to inquisitive young minds.

This experiment shows the natural process of certain chemical reactions. Even very small children will enjoy setting up and watching this experiment. In this natural process captured in a jar or bowl, pretty colored crystals form on pieces of charcoal as a reaction occurs when small amounts of ammonia and bluing are added to the charcoal.

Because a small amount of ammonia is used, there are no bad smells or watery eyes. However, you will want to be careful not to spill any of the ingredients or the solution that you make in this project.

Often, children will see an expensive chemistry set or "crystal garden" in a toy catalog or exclusive toy shop. If your child expresses an interest in such things, you can say: "Let's do our own chemistry experiment. We will make a crystal garden." You and your child can enjoy this project together and it will cost a fraction of one purchased in a store or from a catalog.

With a crystal garden, children will have a wonderful time watching something mysterious and interesting as it grows. The crystal garden will need no care after it is established.

Over a two-day period, you and your children will watch the crystals multiply as the charcoal reacts with the ammonia and laundry bluing.

While you and your child are working together to create the crystal garden, the child will learn to measure, pour, and stir carefully. A sense of curiosity about the nature world also will begin to develop.

Materials and Tools

◇ Measuring spoon
◇ Crystal garden recipe:
  • 6 tablespoons salt
  • 6 tablespoons water
  • 6 tablespoons laundry bluing
  • 1 tablespoon ammonia
  • food coloring
◇ Glass or plastic bowl or large jar
◇ 5 or 6 pieces of charcoal
◇ Spoon

Finding a Place to Work

Choose a work area close to a sink where you can wash your hands and the utensils at the end of this project. Gather your materials and put on old clothes in case a drop of ammonia or bluing splashes away while these liquids are being poured or mixed.

In the bowl, mix the salt, water, laundry bluing, ammonia and food coloring. Let the children decide what color to use. Is one of the children mature enough to stir the mixture while you supervise?

While one of the children stirs the mixture, the other children can arrange the charcoal in the large glass jar or bowl that will house the crystal garden.

Carefully pour the mixture over the charcoal pieces as shown in Fig. 15-1. Then, place the crystal garden in a warm spot—near the kitchen stove, for example. Do not cover.

The Growing Crystal Garden

With the help of the warmth around the crystal garden, the charcoal, ammonia, bluing, and salt react to form beautifully colored crystals that will become more and more visible over the following two days. Within a week, you will have an intriguing crystal garden like the one shown in Fig. 15-2.

While the children are observing the crystals, you can encourage them to draw pictures of what they see. Explain that the different ingredients in the crystal garden are working together—reacting—to form the crystals.

Your children will be delighted with the sparkling crystals. At the same time, you will be teaching them about a simple chemical reaction.

You might carefully lift out one of the pieces of charcoal from the crystal garden so the children can more closely observe the crystals. Place the piece of crystal on a paper towel or piece of cardboard and allow the children to examine the crystals closely. Do you have a magnifying glass or toy microscope? Children will be delighted when they

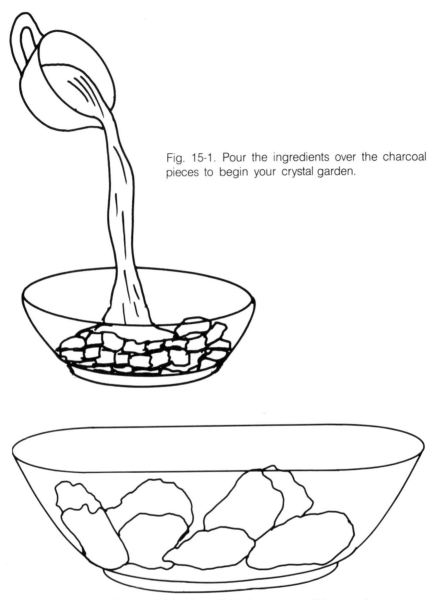

Fig. 15-1. Pour the ingredients over the charcoal pieces to begin your crystal garden.

Fig. 15-2. Your crystal garden will begin to grow within a week.

examine the crystals under magnification. They will be able to see the intricate details of the crystal structure.

With this project, you will be encouraging a child's natural curiosity. In addition to the practice of basic skills such as mixing and pouring, you will be stimulating a child's sense of wonder. This will make future learning experiences easier and more fun.

Weave A
Butter Tub Basket

Age Group: 5 to 10
Time Required: 2 hours

Woven baskets are beautiful works of art but most are hard to weave. Children, as well as adults, find the whole process too much to handle. Weaving itself is a simple procedure as long as there are not a lot of complicated patterns to follow.

Weaving a butter tub basket is easy because the basket has a premade shape and an easy-to-follow pattern. This type of weaving is well suited for children. When you begin weaving a butter tub basket, inquisitive children will want to know the name of the weaving pattern. The name of this kind of weaving is twining.

The little butter tub baskets that you and the children will weave are wonderful gift items and your children will delight in sharing their finished baskets with other family members or with their friends or a special teacher or other significant adult. Also, they can use their finished product in their own bedrooms. Butter tub baskets are perfect for a shelf or dresser in which to store treasured items such as hair barrettes, small toys, or loose change.

This is one of the most challenging of all the projects in this book. Because of the repetitive nature of any type of weaving, even an adult can become bored with a weaving project. Under no circumstances should you let this procedure become tedious for your children. While watching the children do this project, be alert for a heavy sigh or shrugging shoulders. You know the signs that indicate the serious boredom that is fatal to a child's enjoyment of any kind of craft project.

If necessary, to prevent boredom, encourage the children to take turns working on one butter tub basket. While one does a bit of the weaving, the other children can be watching and giving encouragement to the one who is weaving.

While this project develops attention to detail and mechanical skills, you also can use it to develop social skills in your children. Take time to show the children how to give proper encouragement to one another. All too often, siblings learn to criticize and tease. Now, you can teach them to compliment and encourage one another.

Materials and Tools

◇ Plastic tub, such as one containing margarine or butter
◇ Blunt scissors
◇ Black marker or crayon that will mark on the plastic tub
◇ Flexible tape measure
◇ Large-eyed plastic knitting needle
◇ Any assortment of colored yarn

Getting Started

Gather your tools and materials. The plastic tub basic to this project should be as near as your refrigerator. Most butter, margarine, and other spreads come in small plastic tubs. Perhaps, when you are planning a trip to the grocery store, you could look ahead to a day when your child might be seeking a challenging project that will fill several hours. Then, add the word "tubs" to your shopping list so you will remember to look at the many sizes and shapes of spread tubs at your local grocer.

A large-eyed plastic needle and yarn can be found in most sewing or craft shops. The needle and yarn is usually for use in knitting.

With all materials in hand, choose a well-lighted table as your work area. To teach color recognition to preschoolers, encourage your children to separate different colors of yarn into separate piles. Practicing recognizing colors is an excellent preschool activity.

Instruct the children to hold the margarine tub on its side. With your help, have them wrap the flexible tape measure around the top of the tub just under the top edge or lip. Measure the diameter of the tub. Then, using the black marker or crayon, help the children make marks at equal intervals around the top of the tub.

Tell your children to cut down from the top of the tub along each mark using blunt scissors as shown in Fig. 16-1. Encourage them to cut straight lines from the top all the way down the side of the tub to the bottom of the tub. After making the cuts all the way around the tub, set it aside.

Weaving the Yarn

Now, demonstrate how to prepare a piece of yarn for weaving. Begin by laying a piece of yarn on the table in front of you. Using the flexible tape measure, measure out two yards of the yarn. Fold the length of yarn in half and place the loop over one cut section of the margarine tub as shown in Fig. 16-2.

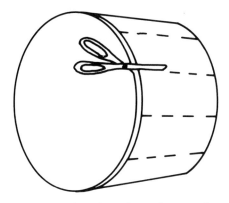

Fig. 16-1. Cut down from the top of the butter tub along each mark using blunt scissors.

Fig. 16-2. Fold the length of yarn in half and place the loop over one cut section of the margarine tub.

Begin criss-crossing the yarn as you work your way around the cut sections of the tub. Bring one length of yarn in front of the tub section while you bring the other length of yarn in back of the cut tub section as shown in Fig. 16-3. Perform this twisting procedure around each cut section all the way around the tub.

You can change yarn colors at any time. When you decide to change colors, loop a new color of yarn around a cut section as shown in Fig. 16-4. Thread the end of the former color into the plastic needle and run the needle under the completed weaving on the outside of the tub as shown in Fig. 16-5. Do the same with the former color yarn hanging on the inside of the tub. This locks the yarn in place.

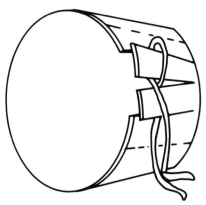

Fig. 16-3. Bring one length of yarn in front of the tub section while you bring the other length of yarn in back of the cut tub section.

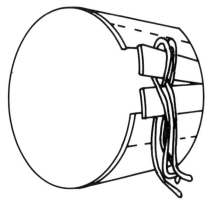

Fig. 16-4. To change colors, loop a new color of yarn around a cut section.

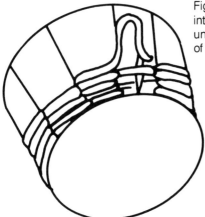

Fig. 16-5. Thread the end of the former color into the plastic needle and run the needle under the completed weaving on the outside of the tub.

Continue the weaving process with each new color. Each time you change colors and lock in the yarn by threading it under the existing loops of yarn, yarn ends will hang out from the place where you threaded them under the existing loops at the bottom of the tub. You can either trim away this excess yarn on the inside and outside of the tub or you can leave it out to create a unique design. Ask the children what they want to do.

As you weave the yarn around the tub, make sure that each layer of yarn sits snugly down on top of the prior layer of yarn. This is a difficult project. Your words of encouragement are vital.

Continue to weave yarn until the entire tub is covered. Work the last layer of yarn snugly under the top edge or lip of the tub. Allow the top edge of the tub to hold all the layers of yarn in place.

When this project is finished, your children will feel tired but proud. With your encouragement, they have persevered in a difficult task. Your positive compliments have built self-esteem and pride in a job well done. And, they will have beautiful, woven baskets. No one will ever know that these baskets began as margarine tubs from the refrigerator.

While you and your children sit back and relax, you can begin thinking of all the possible uses for your beautiful new baskets. These baskets would make a wonderful birthday gift.

The soft yarn will encourage a child's touch and you will soon see each child with a basket spending time on the bed or floor, using the basket as part of important playtime activities and transactions. Do not be surprised if a butter tub basket continues to be a prized possession of each of your children.

Within this project, you have, as a parent, shown to your children how to enjoy a very old craft. The memories will be treasured along with each basket.

Make A
Wind Pinwheel

Age Group: 2 to 10
Time Required: 1 hour

On a warm, sunny day, the breeze can feel so good. However, children are sometimes reluctant to play outside on such nice days. The attractions of television, video games, and other toys often keep children inside.

To encourage outdoor fun, you and your child can make a wind pinwheel. A pinwheel is a simple toy to encourage outdoor play. With a wind pinwheel in hand, your child will love being outside, running across the lawn or in the park, catching the breeze that makes the pinwheel spin, spin, spin.

If you have several young children and each has a pinwheel, you can have simple pinwheel races where the children dash across the lawn pushing the madly spinning pinwheels ahead of them. In a pinwheel race, everyone wins. When your child has burned up some energy and decides to rest, the pinwheel can be stuck in the ground where it will continue to spin as long as there's a breeze to catch.

Inside, a pinwheel can be fun, too. Just take a deep breath, and blow and try to keep the pinwheel going. Without a breeze, your pinwheel can become a festive decoration for a child's bedroom.

On a sunny day, you can make the outdoors look much more attractive. Just say: "It's pinwheel weather." Then, begin gathering the materials you need and soon your children will catch your excitement. You and your children can make a pinwheel in less than an hour. Because this project is so easy and quick, your children will have plenty of time to play with it, outside.

Let's have fun making our wind pinwheel and using it, too.

Materials and Tools

◇ Sheet of typing paper
◇ Transparent tape
◇ Stick or wooden dowel, at least 10 inches long
◇ Thumbtack
◇ Ruler
◇ Pencil
◇ Scissors
◇ Crayons or markers
◇ Glitter

Getting Started

Gather your materials and tools. Because this project can be done just about anywhere, it might be fun to have your children work on this project near a window or even outside on a sunny deck, patio, or porch. They will become more excited as they think about playing outside with their pinwheels.

To begin, ask each child to take a sheet of typing paper and measure a 4-inch square on it as shown in Fig. 17-1. The square can be anywhere on the paper. Watch while the child cuts out the square.

Take your pencil and number each corner of your square: 1 . . . 2 . . . 3 . . . 4 as shown in Fig. 17-2.

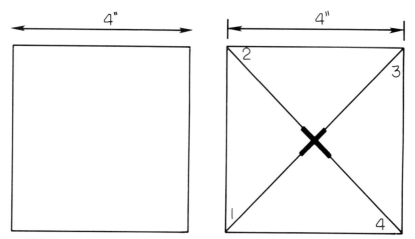

Fig. 17-1. Begin the wind pinwheel with a 4-inch-square piece of typing paper.   Fig. 17-2. Number the corners as shown.

Find the center of the square by drawing a line from corner 1 to corner 3 and from corner 2 to corner 4.

Take a crayon or marker and draw a big, dark X right in the middle of your square along the lines you made from corner to corner. Each leg of the X should be about one inch long. Use your ruler.

Now, encourage your young pinwheel maker to imagine a brightly colored pinwheel spinning in your hand. Use crayons to color both sides of the cut-out square. Use different colors for each section or try a design of spots and stars. Glitter might be a nice addition to a pinwheel, but do not make it too heavy.

From each corner, cut on the lines until you reach the edge of the big, dark X in the center of your square. Stop. Do not cut into the X.

Take corner 1 and fold it into the middle of your square as shown in Fig. 17-3. The point should touch the middle of the square. Tape the corner point in place with a small, square piece of transparent tape. Now, tape corner 2 on top of corner 1 as shown in Fig. 17-4. Do the same thing with corners 3 and 4 as shown in Fig. 17-5. Your wind pinwheel is almost finished.

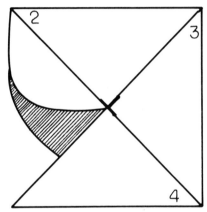

Fig. 17-3. Once cut, fold corner 1 into the middle of the pinwheel and tape it in place.

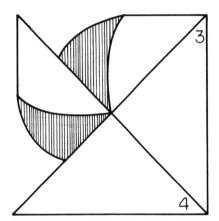

Fig. 17-4. Repeat the process with corner 2.

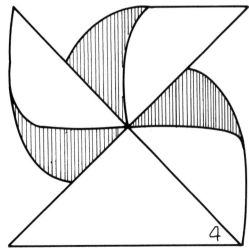

Fig. 17-5. Finish by cutting, folding and taping corners 3 and 4 as shown.

Finishing the Pinwheel

Use markers or crayons to color the pinwheel stick. A few slender strands of ribbon left over from last year's Christmas gift wrappings could be tied to the top of the stick to also move and dance in the wind.

Use the thumbtack to hold the pinwheel to the stick or dowel. Do not push in the thumbtack too far. Your pinwheel should spin freely. Now, with the thumbtack in place, the pinwheel is ready to catch the breeze. Open the door and send your children into the sunshine for some fun.

While your children are outside enjoying the sunshine, the breeze, and the pinwheel, you can relax with pleasant memories of quality time spent making the pinwheel.

Project 18

Make A
Spice Ring

Age Group: 4 to 12

Time Required: 2 hours

On one special occasion, my sister had been making bridal veils, and with the scraps of lace she had created a special gift to give mother and me. The small treasure was a spice ring, a pretty little embroidery hoop with a lace inset, filled with all kinds of good-smelling spices.

Do you remember grandma's kitchen and how good it always smelled when she cooked? Those were the smells of spices. Dried spices also smell very good when used as a "deodorizer sachet." I hung my sachet spice ring on the wall in my bathroom so that room would always smell lovely.

Would you like to make a spice ring for a room in your home, or to give to a relative or friend? It is easy to make, and a special way for you and your children to spend time together. Anyone would enjoy receiving a spice ring as a gift on a special occasion or a special "I love you" surprise.

Materials and Tools
◇ A 4-inch embroidery hoop
◇ 12 inches of lace material
◇ 12 inches of ribbon
◇ 18 inches of lace trim
◇ Glue
◇ Scissors
◇ Small bag of potpourri
◇ Ruler
◇ Teaspoon or measuring spoon

Gathering Your Materials

Load the children in the car and go to a discount store, craft shop, or fabric shop, and ask the clerk for a four-inch embroidery hoop. The hoop is actually two wood hoops, one fitting inside the other. The outside hoop has a small screw mechanism at the top for tightening and untightening the outside hoop.

When material is laid over the inside ring of the embroidery hoop, the outside ring with the screw mechanism is placed over it and the screw is tightened. The tightened outer ring keeps the material from slipping from the hoop when a person embroiders material held in the hoops.

Buy the lace material, ribbon, and lace trim at a fabric shop. Many kinds of potpourri are found in most discount stores and department stores. Allow your children to select their favorite scents.

When you have located all of your tools and materials, find a brightly lit work area with a table. Have your tools and materials at hand, and encourage your children to help you arrange the materials on the table so they are close at hand.

How to Make a Spice Ring

Tell your children to hold the embroidery hoop in both hands, unscrewing the small screw on the outside hoop so the outside hoop can be removed from the inner hoop. See Fig. 18-1.

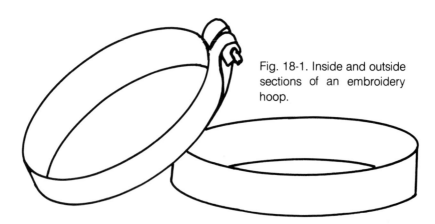

Fig. 18-1. Inside and outside sections of an embroidery hoop.

At this point, you might want to explain to your children why an embroidery hoop is made as it is and what it is normally used for. This will introduce them to new ideas for future hobbies. Hobbies are a source of enjoyment and a release of tension for most adults, but most hobbies or crafts are introduced during childhood. Introduce your children to all kinds of crafts so they can choose one that will continue to be enjoyable in their adult years.

When the hoop rings are separated, lay the two rings aside. Then help the children to measure two, six-inch diameter circles of lace material and cut them out. These two, six-inch diameter circles will hold the spices inside the ring.

After cutting out the circles of lace material, lay one of the circles flat on the table and have your children place three teaspoons of potpourri into the middle of the six-inch square. Then, lift the circle by the edge and lay it over the inner ring of the embroidery hoop.

Lay the other circle of lace material directly on top of the square with the spices as shown in Fig. 18-2. Snap the outer ring over the inner ring of the embroidery hoop. Make sure the lace is pulled tightly over the inner ring so that the material is tight and holding the potpourri as the outer ring is slipped over the material laid over the inner ring.

Fig. 18-2. Lay the other six-inch circle of lace material directly on top of the square with the spices.

With the potpourri spices held between the two squares of lace which is, in turn, held between the two rings of the embroidery hoop, tighten the screw mechanism on the top of the hoop.

Have the children trim the excess lace of the underside of the hoop. Then, lay the hoop face down on the table and tell your children to apply glue all along the outside edge of the hoop. Press the unfinished edge of the lace trim into the glue all along the edge of the back of the hoop. From the opposite side of the ring, the lace edge will appear to be a continuation of the lace inside the ring. Allow the glue to dry for at least fifteen minutes.

Tie the ribbon in a bow around the screw at the top of the embroidery hoop as shown in Fig. 18-3.

Fig. 18-3. Finished spice ring.

Now someone special can enjoy the scent of a lovely spice ring and each time they smell the lovely fragrance, they will think of you and the children. If you have chosen to use the spice ring in your own home, the fragrance will remind you of the precious time you spent together making the spice ring.

Project 19

Make A Macaroni Angel Ornament

Age Group: 4 to 12
Time Required: 3 hours

I love a beautiful Christmas tree filled with lovely ornaments. The most special are the ones that the children have made at school, in Sunday School, at scouts, or with the family.

Each Christmas as we decorate the tree, the children and I discuss each ornament's history before we hang it on the tree. This year, my sister-in-law sent me a special angel ornament that her children had made. It was so beautiful that I want to share it with you and your children.

When the winter holidays approach and stormy weather keeps your children inside, consider making this angel creation. It is simple and inexpensive; it is made of different kinds of macaroni products, a wooden bead, and a tack. You can add pearlized spray paint and oil painted details to make the angel ornament even more delicate and beautiful. The macaroni angel will soar into the hearts of the children who work on this project and you will be creating a family memory that will last forever.

Materials and Tools

◇ White wooden bead, 1 inch in diameter
◇ Small elbow macaroni
◇ Large elbow macaroni
◇ Bow tie noodles
◇ Bead macaroni
◇ Large brass thumbtack
◇ Pearlized spray paint
◇ White glue
◇ Red oil paint
◇ Black oil paint
◇ Small detailing paint brush

◇ Red ribbon, ¹/₄ inch wide, for bow tie
◇ Gold thread
◇ Scissors
◇ Old newspapers
◇ Old clothes

Getting Started

Gather your tools and materials and choose an open-air workplace, or a well-ventilated room. The pearlized spray paint requires a well-ventilated area. All of the tools and materials listed can be found in your local craft store, except the macaroni and noodle products, which can be found in any grocery store. Figure 19-1 shows the bead, the brass thumbtack, and a bow tie noodle. Do you have everything?

Fig. 19-1. Bow tie noodle (a), bead (b), and brass tack (c) needed to begin your macaroni angel ornament.

Tell the children to begin with one large elbow macaroni, which is the body of the angel, and have the children glue one elbow macaroni on each side of the large elbow macaroni at about the place an arm would be located on the body. Refer to Fig. 19-2.

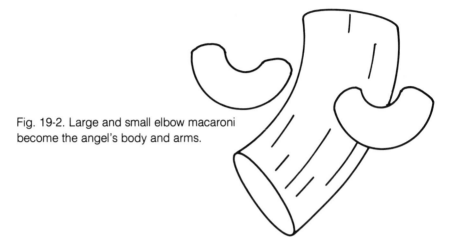

Fig. 19-2. Large and small elbow macaroni become the angel's body and arms.

Waiting for a short time in between each gluing step will set the glue and make handling each newly glued item easier. Trying to glue too quickly will result in an item falling off as your children are gluing on another piece.

Now glue the large white bead on the top of the large macaroni. Spread the glue around the edge of the opening on one end of the macaroni and press the bead into the glue. Tell the children to wait a minute or so until the glue seems firm and the bead does not fall off when they begin to work with the angel body again.

After the glue is dry, have the children glue the bow tie noodle on the back of the angel body. Again, wait for a few minutes for the glue to set. Now, glue the tack onto the two joining small macaronis that represent the arms of the angel. It will appear as though the angel is holding a candle stick when the ornament is completed. Figure 19-3 shows how this step looks when it is completed.

It is now time to glue the angel's hair on the large wooden bead. Open the box of bead macaroni and spread several pieces out on the table for easy access. Then cover the head with a mat of glue, except for the front area of the bead which is the face of the angel. The bead macaroni can be easily pressed into the already prepared glue surface. Have the children apply the bead macaroni two or three at a time as close together as possible. When the entire surface of the bead is covered with the macaroni, wait for the glue to dry.

Fig. 19-3. The completed macaroni angel ornament.

Spray Painting the Macaroni Angel

Tell the children to use the drop cloth or old newspapers to protect the surrounding areas from the spray mist. Then, lay the angel ornament on the protected area and prepare to paint.

First, shake the can vigorously for at least one minute to ensure color uniformity while spraying the ornament. Then, point the opening of the spray button toward the ornament. Make sure the children are holding the can at least 12 to 16 inches away from the ornament. Holding the can this far away keeps the paint from running and clumping. To cover the whole ornament with paint, the ornament will have to be turned and moved while spraying. Consider wearing thin plastic gloves, like the ones worn while coloring hair. Several different sizes are available at most drug stores. If you or your children choose not to wear any protection on your hands, clean your hands with paint thinner when this step is completed, then wash them thoroughly with soap and water. You might want to use hand lotion to protect your and the children's hands from chapping after contact with the harsh paint thinner.

Consult Fig. 19-3 for the details of the angel's face. Have the older children try painting the facial features on the angel's face. If your children are nine or under, have them hand you the paint brush, open the tubes of oil paint, and give suggestions while you paint. Always make your children feel necessary and important to the project's completion.

The angel's mouth is a black oval ring. The eyes are semicircles with wisps of lashes extending from these semicircles. The eyebrows are small slashes above the eyes. On the tip of the tack, paint a red tip. This dash of red makes the tack look like a lighted candle in a candle holder that the angel is carrying.

Now, have the children put a small blob of glue on the top of the angel's head and press a gold thread, which they have doubled and tied in a knot, into the glue. The gold thread will allow the children to hang their prize ornament on the Christmas tree. Now it's time to tie the red ribbon around the neck of the angel in a simple bow. Do not tie the ribbon too tightly or the head of the angel will become unattached.

Christmas will be bright as your angel ornament hangs delicately from the tree.

Project 20

Make A
Musical Maraca

Age Group: 2 to 7
Time Required: 1 hour

A *maraca* is a musical instrument made from a dried, hollow gourd that is often fixed to a wooden handle. Inside the hollow gourd are seeds or pebbles that make a loud, rhythmic, rattling noise when the maraca is shaken. Maracas are often painted in beautiful geometric designs.

Maracas are usually played in pairs and often we see maracas in old cowboy movies where the hero must go "South of the Border" into Mexico on some high adventure. The reason this instrument is seen in Mexico is because it originated in Portugal and is used in Spain, Mexico, and throughout Central and South America.

A maraca is a simple instrument to make and it produces an exciting rhythm. Do your children enjoy music? Making and using one or two maracas is a fun way to introduce children to the idea of a steady beat or rhythm in music. Your children can originate their very own maracas in their own kitchen. They can shake this easy-to-make instrument to the beat of their favorite music.

Children love learning new songs and their eagerness is heightened when they can sing and play along with an adult. If you are not a musician, an album played at home will introduce the music of Spain or Mexico to the children.

With one or two maracas, your children will enthusiastically join into any song with a bright and steady beat. Through home sing-alongs, children will overcome natural shyness. When it comes time to participate in school music classes and programs, they will feel more confident and enjoy the music more.

When you see your child humming a little tune or dancing to some imagined music, you can say: "Let's make a maraca." Then, in just a short time, your child will have an instrument that can be vigorously shaken to the beat of a song. Soon, all the children will be dancing, clapping, and singing.

Materials and Tools

◊ 2 small white Styrofoam cups
◊ Flat wooden stick, such as those used for frozen snacks
◊ Wide, clear packing tape (standard transparent tape is not strong enough for this project)
◊ Several colored markers
◊ Stapler
◊ 5 uncooked, dry beans

Getting Everything You Need

Gather all your tools and materials and try using the kitchen table as your work area. Packages of flat wooden sticks can usually be purchased at a craft store or, possibly, at the grocery store.

Test your colored markers on one of the Styrofoam cups. Certain types of markers contain a permanent paint that dissolves the Styrofoam. Be sure that your markers are safe for Styrofoam.

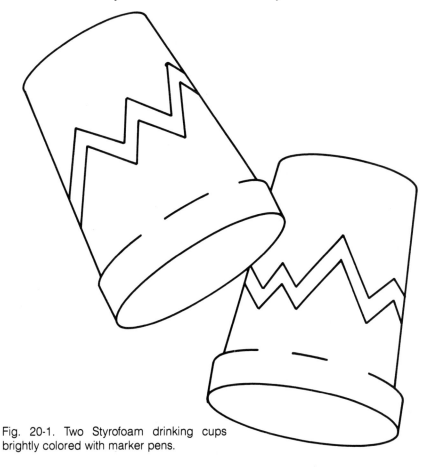

Fig. 20-1. Two Styrofoam drinking cups brightly colored with marker pens.

Can you find a picture of one or two maracas in an encyclopedia, dictionary, or possibly on the cover of a record album of folk music? Look for an article on Mexico or Spain in the encyclopedia. Children will be much more enthusiastic about a project like this when they can see a pair of maracas in use.

Give your children the colored markers and tell them to decorate the outside of two of the Styrofoam cups with designs and pictures. Figure 20-1 shows decorated maracas. Be quick to praise each child's design and color selections.

Before giving the children the dry beans for each maraca, tell them never to put the beans in their mouths, ears, or noses. Then have them place the beans inside one of the cups. Help the younger children count to five as they drop the beans into the cup, one at a time.

Show each child who is making a maraca how to place the larger, open ends of the two decorated cups together and then hold the cups in that position. Either you or another child can use the wide packing tape

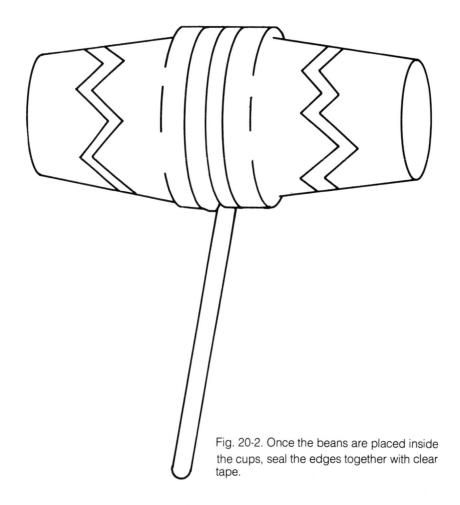

Fig. 20-2. Once the beans are placed inside the cups, seal the edges together with clear tape.

to securely fasten the cups together. If necessary, help each child apply the tape and make sure that none of the beans fall out.

Start with the tape in one spot and run it around the seam where the two cups are held together. However, do not go completely around the cups. Leave a small, untaped opening that is just wide enough to snugly hold the end of a wooden stick as shown in Fig. 20-2.

Finishing the Maraca

Insert the stick into the opening and secure it with two more short strips of clear packing tape, one strip on each side of the stick. The tape is strong enough, and the cups light enough, so that they will not come apart. Figure 20-3 shows completed maracas.

If time permits, make two maracas and have twice as much fun.

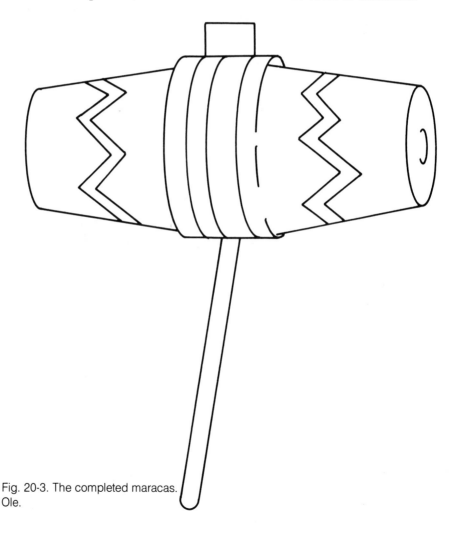

Fig. 20-3. The completed maracas. Ole.

Is everyone ready to experience music with maracas in hand? It's time to turn on your favorite record and shake your maracas to the beat of the music.

Any child will be filled with laughter as the music and the wonderful scratchy noises of the maracas blend into a special rhythm. After you and the children have made the maracas, you will have a wonderful opportunity to show them a world of music that goes far beyond anything heard on radio or television.

Project 21

Make A
Drum

Age Group: 2 to 7

Time Required: 1 hour

When my children were toddlers, they loved to come into my kitchen while I was working. There were two places in my kitchen that my children considered their favorite places to play. One was my drawers of large spoons, spatulas, and other safe utensils, and the other was my cabinet full of pots and pans.

Almost every day, one or more of my children would make their way into the kitchen and begin opening their favorite drawers and cabinets. Soon, a profusion of spoons, spatulas, and other harmless kitchen tools were mingled on the floor with various pots and pans. Then, the music would begin.

My children enjoyed nothing more than the clanging of the spoons and spatulas on the bottoms and sides of the pots and pans. While I enjoyed the uninhibited smiles and shrieks of joy made by the children as they made their music, they often became bored with the kitchen as a concert hall and would try to pick up a favorite pot or pan to move it to another room. Usually, the small child was not strong enough to pick up the item and would, instead, venture from room to room pounding on furniture, walls, and doors with a favorite kitchen utensil.

I soon learned that when one of my toddlers would begin to migrate from the kitchen, this mother had to be swift to follow and return the errant child to the pots and pans. Usually, my firm directions would cause a brief outcry of childish frustration that I termed the "rhythm blues."

After several episodes of pursuing my little drummer boys throughout the house, I realized that some type of drum that was light enough for a 2- or 3-year-old to carry was the answer to their rhythm blues. The child could carry the drum everywhere, enjoying the loud racket, without being tempted to pound on a valuable or thin-skinned item of furniture or decoration. Thus, making a drum was my remedy for their rhythm blues and my on-going worries about my furniture and woodwork.

Do your children experience the rhythm blues? Why not help them make their own drums? Then, show them how they can use the drum anytime without supervision. At the same time, you can teach your children to keep time and rhythm to music.

Making a drum together is great fun and, if you can spend some time with your children to make music together also, you will be adding to their enjoyment of music and showing your love for them. Is there a little drummer boy or girl somewhere in your house right now?

Materials and Tools

◇ 2-pound coffee can with a plastic lid
◇ 2 pieces of construction paper, any color
◇ Colored markers
◇ Glue and glitter, stickers, and other decorations
◇ Blunt scissors
◇ Transparent tape
◇ 2 unsharpened pencils with eraser ends
◇ Patient adults who enjoy the sounds of a child's drum

Getting Started

Children ages 4 to 7 years old can complete almost all of this project alone. When working with these older children, you will only need to supervise the construction of the drum.

Gather your tools and materials. A table in the kitchen, family room, or playroom is the most appropriate work area.

Can you get a large, two-pound coffee can with a plastic lid from your church or perhaps a restaurant or social organization that regularly serves coffee to its members? If you must, buy a two-pound can of your favorite blend and store the coffee in some other tightly sealed container.

Begin by showing the children how to lay out two pieces of colored construction paper to form a cover for the coffee can. Lay the two pieces of construction paper end-to-end and, with the transparent tape, join the ends together. Now, you have one long piece of construction paper. Your piece of construction paper should look like the example shown in Fig. 21-1.

Decorating the Drum Cover

Now, hand out markers or crayons and have each child begin decorating the long piece of construction paper. Encourage vigorous coloring to create strong individual designs. Suggest the use of glitter, stickers, or other special decorations that will make each drum unique. Young children will enthusiastically plunge into a coloring project where they have complete creative freedom.

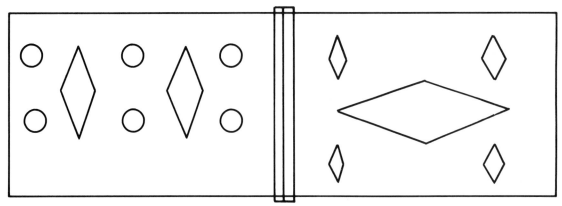

Fig. 21-1. Decorating construction paper for the coffee can drum.

When each child has finished coloring and decorating the drum cover, show them how to wrap the long piece of decorated construction paper around the coffee can as shown in Fig. 21-2.

If necessary, trim the top or bottom edge so the construction paper fits the coffee can perfectly. Then, tape the construction paper to the top and bottom edges of the can so the edges are smooth and the construction paper is firmly attached to the can. Small hands will have trouble cutting and taping the construction paper to the edges of the can, so intervene by trimming after they have done all they can do, then continue to help by taping over any places they might miss. Always supply encouraging words and happy smiles, too.

Now, the children can pop the plastic lid on the can/drum. This plastic lid forms the top for a child's drum. Figure 21-3 shows a completed drum. Hand out two unsharpened pencils with eraser ends that will work nicely as drum sticks.

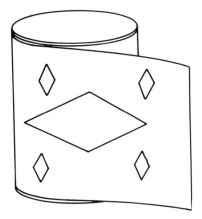

Fig. 21-2. Wrapping the coffee can sides with the construction paper.

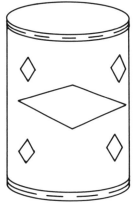

Fig. 21-3. The completed coffee can drum.

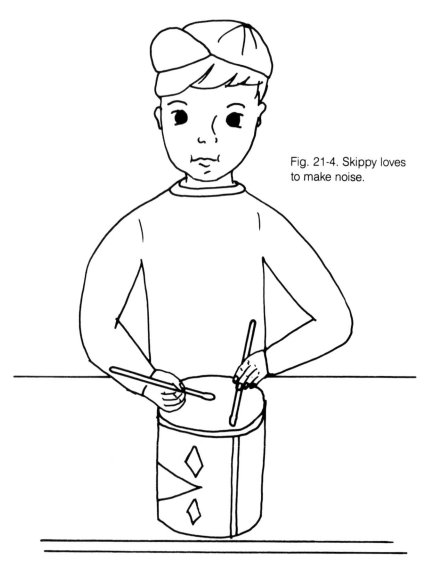

Fig. 21-4. Skippy loves to make noise.

Each child's drum is now ready to use. It is a lasting, durable toy they can enjoy again and again. Skippy is shown enjoying his drum in Fig. 21-4.

If you have time, you might take the children to the public library and find several children's books about drums and little drummer boys and girls. Perhaps a record of rousing march music also could be checked out for enjoyment at home. Each time you encourage the children to get involved with music in some way, you are planting seeds that could blossom into a lifelong interest in an instrument. You are providing the opportunity for self-discovery and the lifelong enjoyment of music in all its many forms.

Make A Musical Instrument: A Bucket Bass

Age Group: 4 to 7

Time Required: 1 hour

When my children were very small, I began playing the guitar. They loved watching me pluck the strings and listen to the instrument produce beautiful tones. It was all I could do to keep them from sneaking into my room to strum the strings. Often, each child would ask: "Mommy, I want to play the guitar. Let me hold it and play the strings." They were not satisfied when I held the guitar with them but they were too small to hold the guitar alone. What could I do?

The children needed a musical instrument that was just the right size and shape for easy handling by pudgy little hands. The instrument had to be inexpensive and rugged, easy to fix, and yet it had to give off a loud sound that would be satisfying to my budding young musicians.

After several days of thinking and asking the children to be patient, I began to despair of ever having an idea . . . until one evening when I was watching a humorous program on television. A "hillbilly band" was playing a rousing tune and I noticed, in the back, a grinning fellow who was vigorously plucking away on a single string that stretched from the bottom of an overturned wash tub under his foot to the top of an old broom handle. To the beat of the music, this country bass player was "plucking and grinning."

Later that night, after I had put the children to bed and sang several songs to them, my middle boy piped up and again asked: "Momma, when are we going to get a guitar so we can play?" Now, I could answer him. I said: "Tomorrow, we'll make you a special instrument that you can play."

The next day, we talked and planned and gathered materials for our first "bucket bass." A bucket bass is a single-stringed instrument with a deep sound like a bass fiddle. You can make the bucket bass from a metal bucket, a broom handle, and a guitar string. A child of almost any age can play the bucket bass by moving the broom handle back and forth beside the bucket that is held to the floor by the child's foot. Moving the broom handle tightens or loosens the string that makes the tones produced by the bucket bass higher or lower.

Now, when your children want to make music, you can say: "Let's make a bucket bass together." This bass is not costly or hard to play and it is simple to make.

Materials and Tools

◇ Small metal bucket
◇ Guitar string
◇ Wooden broom handle
◇ An ice pick or an awl
◇ Hammer
◇ Hand saw

Getting Started

Gather your materials and tools. A metal bucket is the best item to use for the bucket bass because the sloping sides and wider top of a bucket form a stable platform for a little foot when the bucket is turned upside down and placed on the floor. You will find a metal bucket at a hardware store.

You can find the wooden broom handle at the hardware store. One end of the broom handle should be flat and the other end could be either flat or rounded. If both ends are rounded, ask someone at the hardware store to cut off about $1/2$ inch of the broom handle to make a nice, flat end.

A guitar string made of nylon works well and such a string can be purchased from a music store. Be sure that the guitar string you buy has a metal or plastic ball at one end of the string. This ball will hold the end of the string inside the bucket when you put your instrument together. When you go to the music store, take your children with you and encourage them to think about the wonderful world of music.

STOP The first assembly step is one that you should do while your children watch. You will be using the awl or ice pick and the hammer to poke a hole in the center of the bottom of the bucket. Use the garage or basement floor as your work area. Caution: The awl and hammer are unsafe for younger children.

To make the hole, first look at the metal or plastic ball on the end of the guitar string. Compare the ball to the diameter of the awl or ice pick you will be using. Imagine how far through the bottom of the bucket the awl will have to go to make the right sized hole. The hole you make must be smaller than the ball on the end of the guitar string so that the string will stay attached to the bucket.

To make the hole, turn your bucket upside down on the solid concrete floor. Place the point of the awl or ice pick directly in the center of the bottom of the bucket as shown in Fig. 22-1. Gently tap the handle of the awl with the hammer until the point of the tool punches through the bottom of the bucket. Do not strike the tool too hard or you might make a hole that is too large to hold the ball at the end of the guitar string.

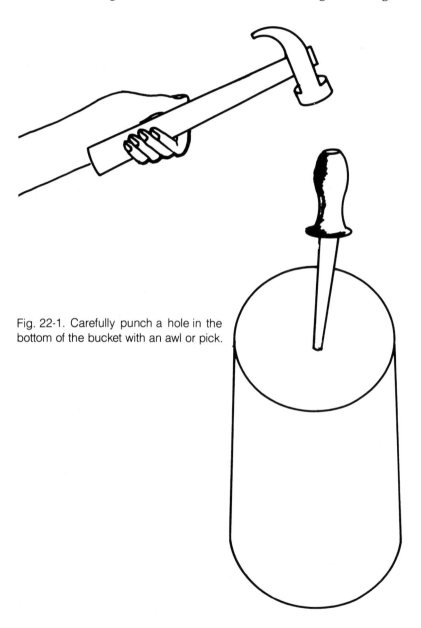

Fig. 22-1. Carefully punch a hole in the bottom of the bucket with an awl or pick.

Take the broom handle and find the rounded top end. You must make a hole through the rounded top end of the broom handle for the opposite end of the guitar string. Lay the broom handle down on the floor and place the point of the awl into the wood of the broom handle about one inch down from the top of the broom handle. With the hammer, again gently tap the awl until you drive it through the broom handle, making a hole in the handle. Drive the awl straight through the broom handle as shown in Fig. 22-2 and do not wiggle it back and forth a lot because this could crack the broom handle.

If you have an electric drill and a small drill bit for wood, you can also drill the hole through the broom handle.

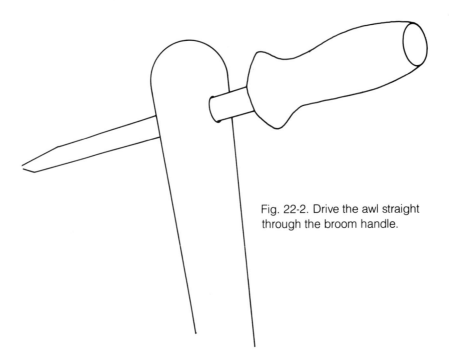

Fig. 22-2. Drive the awl straight through the broom handle.

Stringing the Instrument

Now, it is time to string the bucket bass. Are the children getting excited? Guitar strings with a metal or plastic ball on the end are the easiest to work with because you do not have to tie the end of the string to attach it to the bucket.

Take the end of the guitar string without the ball and then thread the guitar string through the hole in the bottom of the bucket from the inside of the bucket as shown in Fig. 22-3. This is an excellent activity to teach coordination to young children.

After threading the guitar string through the hole, have one of the children tug on the string to make sure it will stay in place.

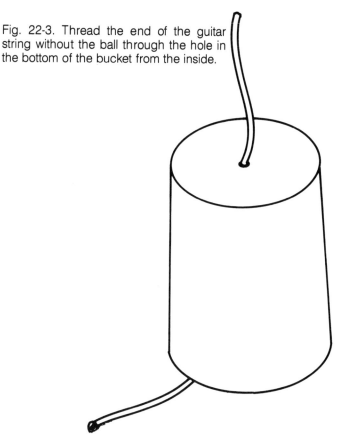

Fig. 22-3. Thread the end of the guitar string without the ball through the hole in the bottom of the bucket from the inside.

Place the end of the broom handle firmly on the floor beside the bucket. Then, hold the broom handle straight up. Thread the top of the guitar string through the broom handle and pull all excess string through the hole so that the guitar string is tight between the bottom of the bucket and the top of the broom handle. Tie the extra string in a knot around the top of the broom handle to hold it firmly.

Now, the bucket bass is ready to play. Who will be first to try it? Skippy is shown playing his bucket bass in Fig. 22-4.

Now, it is time for your children to experiment with their new string bass. Show them how to place a foot on the edge of the bucket and then hold the broom handle down on the floor near the bucket. Soon, each child will discover that changing the string's tone is as easy as moving the top of the broom handle back and forth over the bucket.

Each child will enjoy the fun provided by a bucket bass. Do you have time now to sing and clap along with the child? If you play a musical instrument, join the child in an impromptu duet. You will be stimulating the child's natural love of music and you will be sharing a special and loving time together.

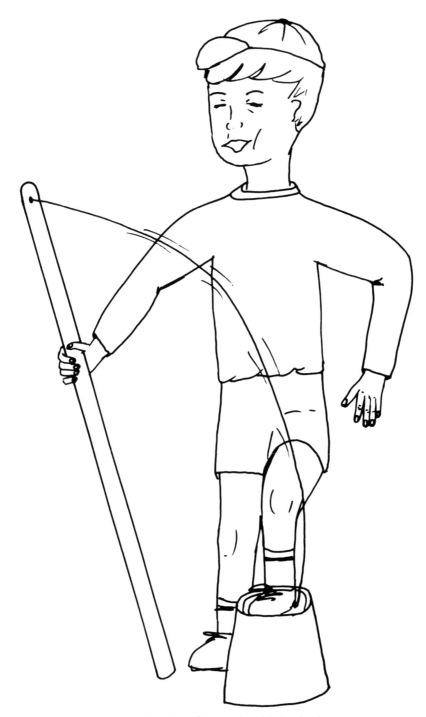

Fig. 22-4. Skippy plays his bucket bass.

Project 23

Make A Ukulele

Age Group: 4 to 7
Time Required: 1 to 2 hours

Children love to pretend. Pretending is an important exercise. Through pretend roles in playtime fantasies, children practice and learn many important rules of behavior and they can explore their own developing personalities.

Maybe your children enjoy pretending they are music stars? Although a tennis racquet or baseball bat might be an adequate substitute for a musical instrument, a pretend concert will be much more real and fun when the children have an instrument to use while they pretend.

In this project, we will make something as simple as a cardboard tissue box strung with rubber bands that makes sounds like a real stringed instrument. Your children will enjoy assembling their very own ukulele.

A ukulele is a stringed musical instrument closely resembling, but smaller than, a guitar with four strings. The word *ukulele* is a Hawaiian word: *uku*, meaning flea, and *lele*, meaning jumping. Have you ever seen a native Hawaiian play a ukulele? The Hawaiian's fingers fairly fly as they rapidly play the ukulele.

When you help your children assemble this tissue box ukulele, you will be helping them gain valuable basic skills, such as being able to follow directions. When the project is finished the children will have an instrument that they can strum in their pretend concerts. Now, gather the little ones, make the ukulele, and watch as their fingers fly over the strings.

Materials and Tools

◇ Tissue box
◇ 4 long, strong rubber bands
◇ Piece of heavy cardboard, 9 inches long

◇ Piece of yarn, 40 inches long
◇ Sharp cutting tool
◇ Construction paper
◇ Colored markers
◇ Blunt scissors
◇ Glue

Getting Started

To begin, gather your materials and decide on a suitable work area.

Find a broad, low, and wide cardboard tissue box with an oval opening in the center of the top like the one shown in Fig. 23-1. Often, such boxes of tissues are presented as being for a man's dresser and the right kind of box can be spotted in the grocery store by looking for a masculine design of duck decoys or old parchment maps on the outside of the box.

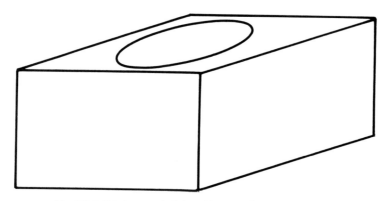

Fig. 23-1. Start your ukulele with a cardboard tissue box.

The oval opening is important as an outlet for the sounds of the ukulele so, if the box does not have an oval opening, cut one in the box with the cutting tool.

Caution: Always handle sharp cutting tools and do not trust young children to safely use such items. Often, a child will beg for a chance to gain your attention and approval by asking to use the razor knife, but say no.

Tell your children to choose several pieces of construction paper in the color that they want to make their instruments. Place the tissue box on the construction paper and show the children how to trace around the box with a pencil. Trace each side of the tissue box onto the construction paper and allow the children to use the blunt scissors to cut out these pieces of construction paper.

With the glue, stick each piece of construction paper to the correct side of the tissue box. Before gluing on the top piece of construction paper, lay it onto the tissue box and make an estimate of the size of the sound hole on top of the box. Then, cut out that area of the top piece of construction paper. Do not cover the oval opening in the top of the tissue box because the opening allows the sound to resonate from inside the box.

Adding the Strings

Add the strings of the ukulele. The rubber bands that will serve as strings should be strong enough so the children can stretch them the length of the tissue box. Each rubber band must cross the center opening of the tissue box.

Every stringed instrument has a support piece that holds the strings up away from the body of the instrument so the tones are clear and resonant. This support piece is called the bridge. You can make a bridge for your ukulele by cutting out a piece of cardboard that is 1 inch wide and just as long as the oval opening in the top of your ukulele.

Have the children fold this cardboard support piece in half and cut four small V-shaped slits into the folded edge. Does your bridge look like the one shown in Fig. 23-2? These slits are for the rubber bands to rest in. Now, show the children how to apply a little glue along the opposite edges of the bridge. Slip the bridge under the rubber bands at a point near to the oval opening. Press the bridge onto the top of the ukulele and have the children lift the rubber bands and allow each one to rest in one of the slits cut in the bridge.

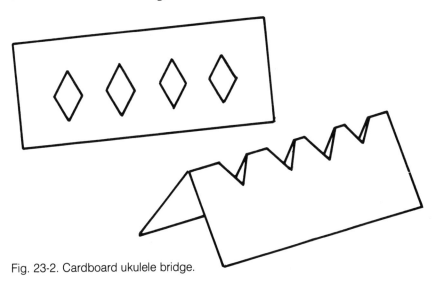

Fig. 23-2. Cardboard ukulele bridge.

Making the Neck

Every successful ukulele must have a neck for eager little hands to hold. To make a neck, cut a piece of cardboard from a sturdy box or piece of cardboard scrap. Cutting thick cardboard is an adult activity because the cutting tool is sharp and could slip in tender, little hands.

The piece of cardboard that you cut for the neck of the ukulele should be nine inches long and two inches wide. Also, cut two small pieces of cardboard about 5 inches long and ¹/₂ inch wide. These pieces will form the tuning pegs of your ukulele.

Lay the neck piece flat on a table and glue or tape the two other cardboard pieces onto the neck piece. Place the pegs about 2 inches apart and about 2 inches from the top of the neck.

Glue the other end of the neck piece onto the back of the tissue box so that it covers the rubber bands as they encircle the tissue box body of the ukulele. Apply a thin coating of glue all along the back of the tissue box and then press the cardboard neck piece down over the rubber bands to make contact with the glue. Place a heavy weight, such as a book, on the neck piece where it covers the rubber bands. Set the ukulele aside to allow the glue to dry. When the glue is dry and the neck feels sturdy, you are finished (Fig. 23-3).

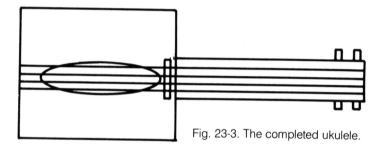

Fig. 23-3. The completed ukulele.

You can add a yarn strap to the ukulele by simply punching one small hole in the base of the ukulele. Then, push a piece of yarn through the hole until the end of the yarn is seen through the oval hole under the strings. Slip your fingers between the strings and grasp the yarn, pull it out for a length and then tie a knot in the end of it. Draw the knot back inside the ukulele by gently pulling on the other end. To complete the yarn strap, tie the other end of the yarn around the neck of the ukulele near the cardboard tuning pegs.

Any child with a ukulele will enjoy many hours of fun. Imagination will take the child to a concert stage in some warm tropical climate where eager natives will gather for a concert of popular music. You can stimulate a child's imagination by taking the time necessary to go to the public library and check out a record or cassette bearing ukulele music from the Hawaiian Islands.

You might even have a future rock star (Fig. 23-4).

Fig. 23-4. Skippy joins the immortal ukulele players of all time.

Project 24

Make A Braided Yarn Belt

Age Group: 8 to 12

Time Required: 2 hours

When I was in the fourth grade, the "in" thing to do was to make braided belts, necklaces, and bracelets. Girls and boys would labor to make the pretty items then give them in friendship to their favorite person. I remember laboring long and hard on a braided belt that I gave as a Christmas gift to my best girlfriend.

Not long ago, my nine-year-old daughter, Nikki, came home from school and began making a "friendship" bracelet for a special friend. When Nikki was finished, I told her about how I had made a braided belt when I was just a little bit older than she was. Nikki asked: "Can we make a braided belt together, mommy?"

Braided items make beautiful, colorful gifts and add pretty accents to any wardrobe. How would your children like to make a braided belt from yarn to give as a gift to a friend or to wear with their jeans or skirts?

The yarn is braided and looped to fit the waist of the wearer. One size fits all and you have done the work yourself. Give this project a try and just see how much fun you can have with plain old yarn.

Materials and Tools

◇ 144 pieces of yarn, in colors of your choice, each piece about 12 feet long
◇ Scissors

Organizing the Yarn

Separate the piece of yarn, then tie them all together, leaving 24 inches of yarn loose on the end. Separate the sections by color in groups of 48 pieces. Now, begin braiding.

Braid until you come to the point that there is 24 inches left on the other end, as shown in Fig. 24-1. It is important to leave 24 inches on each end so there is enough yarn for the tails that hang.

If you use red, blue, and green, there will be 48 pieces of red, 48 pieces of blue, and 48 pieces of green, all coming from the mass of tied yarn. Cross the red yarn on the right side over the middle blue pieces. Then, pass the green yarn on the left side over the already overlapped red pieces of yarn. Continue this overlapping of colors.

Regardless of their position, the overlapping procedure would be the same all the way to the stopping point, 24 inches from the other end.

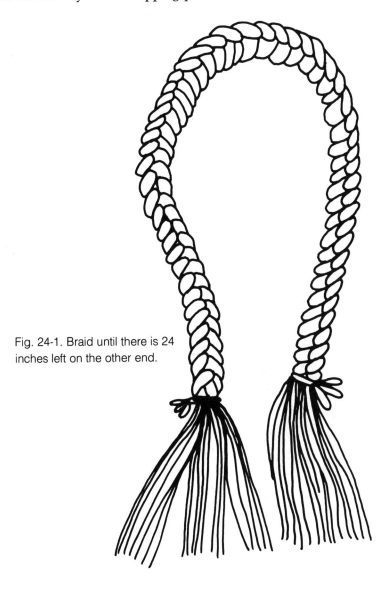

Fig. 24-1. Braid until there is 24 inches left on the other end.

Then tie off the braiding with a small piece of yarn. If you have ever braided hair, pretend to do the same thing, only this time you will be braiding yarn.

When the children have finished braiding the sections of yarn, fold the braided section in half so there is a loop on one end and all the loose sections of yarn on the other end. Temporarily tie the belt at the point where the loose sections meet.

Tell the children to divide the loose pieces of yarn into 4 sections with 12 pieces of yarn in each section as shown in Fig. 24-2. Have them braid each of those 4 sections halfway down and tie them tightly. Divide the remaining yarn into 4 sections again with 3 pieces of yarn in each section and braid again. When each of these sections are braided, tightly tie the ends with a piece of yarn.

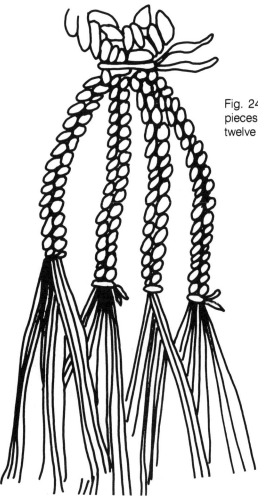

Fig. 24-2. Divide and braid the loose pieces of yarn into four sections with twelve pieces of yarn in each section.

Now, go back and wrap the children's choice of yarn around each place the belt has been tied off. This will secure the strength of the sections so they will remain braided. Wrap the yarn around and around several times, then tie a secure knot so the wrapping will hold. Use a needle and thread the end of the wrapping yarn to make the knot if necessary. Then the knot will be secure.

The belt is ready to wear. Put the belt around one of the children's waists and push the braided hanging sections through the loop on the other side. Allow the smaller braided sections to hang in front. See how Skippy is wearing his belt in Fig. 24-3. Your children will enjoy wearing the belt themselves or giving the belt to one of their close friends.

The same braiding technique can be applied to make necklaces or bracelets.

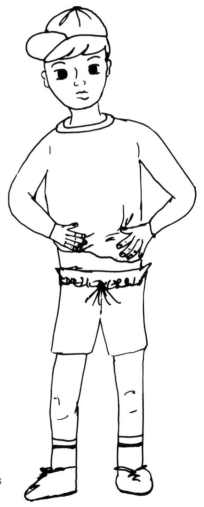

Fig. 24-3. Skippy proudly wears his braided yarn belt.

Make A Baby Toy: Spools on a String

Age Group: 5 to 7

Time Required: 2 hours

When my children were small, one of their favorite toys was a long string of colored sewing thread spools strung on a long, sturdy shoe string. The large spools and shoelace were easy for tiny hands to grasp. The wooden spools, painted with a safe enamel, could be tasted by a toddler, but were large enough to discourage a child from constantly having them in the mouth.

The spool train was the perfect toy to encourage good coordination in tiny hands and it attracted a toddler's attention to detail. It could be carried by one tiny hand or dragged like a pet puppy on a leash. It often served as a security blanket and comforter.

Have you dealt with the jealousy felt by an older child toward a baby brother or sister? Often, an older child will say: "I don't like baby." When this happens, now you can say: "I know just what we can do together. Let's make a toy for the baby." By doing this project together with your older child, you will be expressing love for the older child and together you will be showing your love for the younger child. When your older child sees the happiness expressed by the toddler, he will feel the warmth of love.

Spools on a string are a wonderful teaching toy for older babies. They are also great fun to make. Consider having an older child make and give this hand-made toy to a baby brother or sister. You and your children will spend two pleasant hours together making this toy that teaches love to all who make it.

This will be a special gift from an older sibling to a younger one. Try to keep this project a secret while you and the older children are working on it. Keeping it a secret assures a nice surprise for the younger child and also allows the older children to enjoy the spool toy for a while after they finish making it.

Materials and Tools

◇ 7 empty wooden sewing thread spools
◇ 1 extra long shoestring
◇ 1 or more colors of nontoxic spray enamel
◇ 1 or more colors of nontoxic enamel paint
◇ Rubber gloves (for spray painting)
◇ Paintbrushes
◇ Masking tape
◇ Old clothes or a paint smock
◇ Old newspapers

Getting Started

You must select a brand of nontoxic enamel paint that will dry to a finish safe for a toddler. If you have enamel paints at home, take the time to study all labels with the child who will be making the toy. Read the big words and explain how the paint must be the right kind for a baby toy.

If you must go to a store to buy the enamel, first sit down with the child who will be making the toy and talk about the colors to be used for the spools. Perhaps you could get out a box of crayons or colored markers and have the child pick his favorite colors. Will all the spools be the same color? Will one spool be red, one green, and another yellow? Let your child's imagination determine the colors.

Do you have seven large wooden thread spools? Before spending money on the spools, consider asking for spools from a friend or relative who might be in a "sewing circle." If necessary, such spools can be purchased at a craft store or hobby shop.

Now, it is time to go to the store and buy the enamel and spools. Be sure to take your older child with you to help select the colors of paint. Any discount store should carry enamel paint. Both the spray paint and the small cans of brush-on enamel must have a label stating whether or not the paint is toxic. Be sure to look for a label reading something like this: "These enamels are nontoxic when dry making them safe for all household use, including toys and baby furniture." When you see this label, you will know that the enamel paint is safe for this project. Do not use any other type of paint.

After finding the enamel at home or buying the right colors at the store, you are ready to begin painting the spools, just like Skippy and his dad in Fig. 25-1. Carefully choose a work area. Because you will be using spray paint, this step must be done in a workroom or garage where it is safe to use spray paint. Put on your old clothes. An adult's old shirt or blouse makes an excellent paint smock for a child.

Spray Painting the Spools

Put down your old newspapers to catch the paint spray. Tell your children to set the spools up in a row on the newspaper-covered surface.

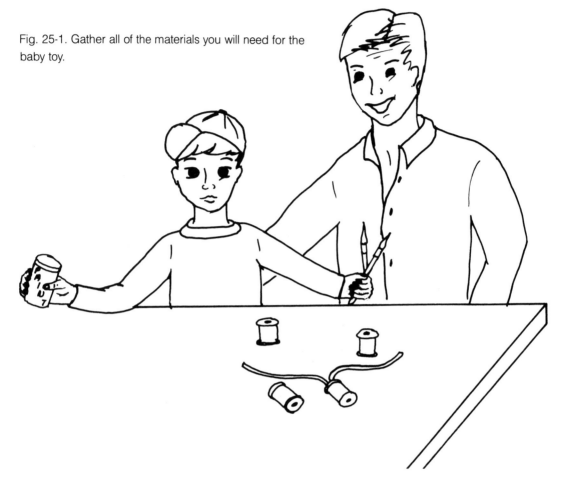

Fig. 25-1. Gather all of the materials you will need for the baby toy.

STOP Spray painting is difficult to do evenly and the fumes are toxic, so you must do this step. Put on the rubber gloves and shake the spray can of enamel vigorously. Ask the children to stand back so the fumes will not bother them. Hold the can 12 to 16 inches from the spools when spraying.

Spray each of the spools the color your children have chosen. Spray the sides and top of each spool with several long, smooth strokes that put several light coats of paint on each spool. Allow the spools to dry for about 15 minutes. This is the perfect time for you and your older child to spend some quiet time together. Perhaps, you could look at the older child's baby pictures.

After about 15 minutes, you must carefully check to see if the paint has dried. Do not let eager little hands get into wet paint. If the enamel is dry, allow the older child to turn the spools over. Then, you must paint the bottom surface areas of each spool. Wait another 15 minutes for this part of each spool to dry.

Now is the time to paint. Do you have a work bench or old table where you and the children can sit down together with the cans of enamel? Cover the table with newspapers, give each child one of the painted spools, and begin discussing how the child would like to decorate it.

Open one of the small cans of enamel paint and show the children how to paint each of the spools with a brush as shown in Fig. 25-2. Tell them to use their imaginations and encourage the children to use several different colors on one spool to make many different designs.

Figure 25-2 will give you an idea how even the smallest designs are creative. Encourage and praise each of their efforts. Dots, lines, splotches, or squiggles make the spools colorful and interesting. Allow another 15 minutes for these designs to dry.

Fig. 25-2. Paint each of the spools with a brush.

When the spools are completely dry, tell the children it is time to string the spools on the lone shoestring. First, let one of the children tie a sturdy knot in one end of the shoestring. Encourage the child to leave some of the shoe string extending out from the knot so that it can be tied to the other end to form a necklace if the children want to. However, they must tie this first knot in one end of the shoe string so the spools will not slide off.

Begin placing the spools on the shoestring as shown in Fig. 25-3. When all the spools have been placed on the shoestring, have the children either tie both ends of the shoelace together loosely to make a necklace, or tie another knot in the other end of the shoelace to hold the spools in place in a long line.

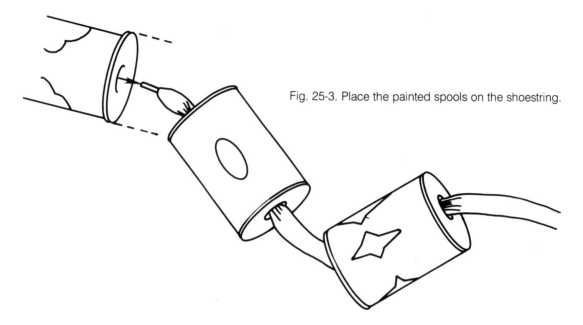

Fig. 25-3. Place the painted spools on the shoestring.

Always tie all knots in the shoe string loosely so they can be easily untied. The toddler who will receive this toy gift will either be able to wear the spools like a necklace or play with the spool toy like a long chain or train. Also, by untying one end knot, the toddler can be encouraged to unstring and restring the spools. This type of activity teaches coordination in tiny hands.

Before giving the spool toy to the toddler, let the older children who have worked so hard enjoy it (Fig. 25-4). This gives them a chance to savor their hard work and appreciate the project.

After they have worn the spools for some time, you might encourage them to place the spool toy in a box and wrap it up as a gift for the baby or toddler. Have the older child give the toddler the gift and help unwrap it while you stand back and watch the joy and love.

With this simple project, you and your older children have spent time together making a special teaching toy while you've taught your older children to share and care about a younger sibling or other young relative or friend.

The older children will be thrilled when they see the joy when the younger child first sees the brightly colored spools. With a wide smile and bright eyes, baby brother or sister will shriek with joy and shake and toss the spool toy.

Fig. 25-4. Skippy models the completed spools-on-a-string baby toy—hoping his friends don't see him.

Make A Papier-Mâché Hand Puppet

Age Group: 5 to 10

Time Required: Several hours over two afternoons

My husband and I have spent several enjoyable weekend afternoons at home being entertained by puppet shows staged for us by our children. In addition to writing a simple script, the children used household materials to make different kinds of homemade puppets.

As each of my children got old enough to try this type of activity, I encouraged them to create one or more puppets for simple shows. This kind of activity helps children be creative and imaginative.

If your children enjoy creative activities in which they can use their imagination, try making just one simple hand puppet from materials you probably have in your own home. The process is easy but fun, and the hours of playtime it creates for your children is satisfying for you, too. The basic design of this puppet can be changed by creative children to produce a wide range of different characters for all types of puppet shows.

A small degree of patience is required because the papier-mâché used to make each puppet's head must be allowed to dry for at least 48 hours before the head can be painted. If your children would like to stage a weekend puppet show for family and friends, begin making the puppets on a Monday or Tuesday afternoon. The children will have plenty of time to complete the puppets, plan a program, and rehearse it.

What is a puppet show without a stage for the actors and actresses? If you have a large work area and sufficient time, you also might consider doing another project found in this book: making a puppet stage. Both of these projects use papier-mâché and common tools.

While the papier-mâché is drying, you and the children can be preparing a script for the show and rehearsing the lines to be said by the actors and actresses. You will be surprised by the subjects that children will cover in a puppet show. If you would like to know more about your children, encourage them to create an entire puppet show.

Materials and Tools

◇ Papier-mâché recipe:
  • 1 cup flour
  • 1¹/₂ cups warm water
◇ Pie pan or other type of wide, low bowl
◇ Stirring whisk or spatula
◇ Old newspapers
◇ Blunt scissors
◇ Glue
◇ String
◇ Small balloon
◇ Two old handkerchiefs or other pieces of cloth
◇ Toilet paper tube
◇ Needle and thread
◇ White tempera paint
◇ Other paint colors, such as a flesh tone

Planning a Puppet

While you and the children gather all of the materials and tools, begin discussing the kind of puppet you will make first. Will it be a baseball player or a world famous explorer? Will the puppet be the school yard bully or an imaginary friend? Children love sharing their ideas.

Find a convenient place to do this project. A good place to work is in the kitchen or another place near a sink and a table or a wide countertop.

Making the Puppet's Head

A balloon will form the pattern for the puppet's head. Ask the children if they want a big puppet or a small one. Ask them to show you the size of their puppet's head with their hands or by tracing a circle on a piece of paper. The size of the balloon determines the size of the puppet's head.

Begin making the puppet's head by asking for a volunteer to blow up the balloon to the size indicated by the children. If one of the children is able to blow up the balloon, give quick and genuine praise for a job well done. However, be prepared to help out by blowing up the balloon after several valiant efforts by the children. Tie the opening of the balloon shut with a string that can be untied later.

Place the balloon over one end of the cardboard tube from a roll of toilet tissue. Place the balloon so that the end that you tied with the string is seated down inside the cardboard tube. With a marker, draw on the balloon around the edge of the tube. This mark tells you how far down to bring the papier-mâché when you cover the balloon.

Now, mix the papier-mâché paste. Your children will enjoy this pro-cess because they can do all the mixing themselves without your help.

The only help they might need is in measuring out the ingredients. The recipe makes enough for one puppet. The recipe can be doubled or tripled if needed.

Let the children pour the flour and water into the pie pan and then show them how to blend it together with the stirring whisk. Tell the children to be sure the mixture is thick and smooth. If it does not seem thick enough, add more flour until the mixture is fairly stiff, not soupy.

Have the children cut the newspaper into long thin strips, about two inches wide and ten inches long. When they have quite a few strips, tell them to dip the strips into the papier-mâché mix. Monitor the amount of papier-mâché on each strip. You might have to squeeze out the excess paste because too much paste will cause the strip to slide from the balloon rather than adhere to it.

Have the children apply the strips of gooey newspaper to the balloon by wrapping the strips around the balloon until the whole balloon, down to the marker line, is hidden by the wet strips. Several layers of these strips form the shape of a head for the puppet (Fig. 26-1). The thickness of the papier-mâché layer determines the rigidity of the head.

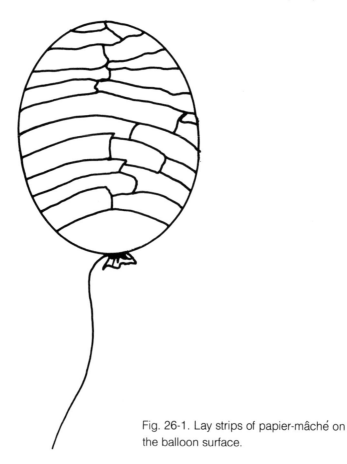

Fig. 26-1. Lay strips of papier-mâché on the balloon surface.

Be sure that the papier-mâché strips come down just over the marker line. This is important, because after the papier-mâché has dried, you will remove the balloon by deflating it. Then, you will mount the head shape on the cardboard tube. By bringing the papier-mâché down just over the marker line, you are ensuring that the head shape will fit snugly on the cardboard tube.

When the balloon is covered, set it aside to dry.

Allow the papier-mâché to dry for about a half hour while you sew the body of the puppet. The puppet's body is made by laying the two handkerchiefs (or other squares of cloth) flat on the table. Sew up the sides with the needle and thread or sewing machine to form a simple cloth tube. Leave one end of the tube completely open and leave just a small space open at the other end of the cloth tube for the cardboard neck tube of the puppet. Reinforce the area on either side of the neck opening by tying the thread in a knot. The bottom of the handkerchiefs is left open for the hand of your budding young puppeteers to enter and control the movement of the puppet.

In about a half hour, the papier-mâché head shape should be solid enough that you can deflate the balloon by untying the string. Pull the balloon out of the head shape and, if necessary, gently make the hole opening large enough to insert the end of the cardboard tube into the head shape about two inches. Do not insert the tube too far because the puppeteer will need several inches of the tube as a handle to maneuver the puppet's head. Apply a little glue around the edges of the area where the tube is inserted so the tube cannot fall out when the puppet is completed.

The papier-mâché must dry for about two days before you paint the head, so set it in a safe place until it is completely dry.

Painting the Puppet's Face

When the papier-mâché is thoroughly dry, you can let your children paint the head with a base coat of white tempera paint. Handle the puppet head by the cardboard neck tube. In about ten minutes, the white paint is dry, so now encourage the children to paint the eyes, nose, mouth and hair with different colors of tempera paint. Your children will enjoy decorating the head of each puppet.

Are there other ways to decorate a puppet's head? Each child will have a little different idea to contribute. This is the fun. Allow the paint to dry for 15 minutes while you and the children discuss other ways to make the puppet look realistic.

Insert the cardboard tube "neck" of the puppet into the handkerchief body that you made earlier (Fig. 26-2). Position the body and head by having one of the children stick a hand into the puppet and hold the neck tube. Apply a thin line of white glue around the puppet's neck and hold the cloth to the glue until it begins to dry. Set the puppet aside for

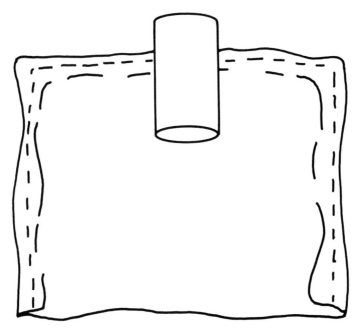

Fig. 26-2. Insert the cardboard tube "neck" of the puppet into the handkerchief body that you made earlier.

about 15 minutes more to allow the glue to finish drying. The puppet should now be completed and ready for a starring role in the children's own puppet show (Fig. 26-3).

After so much hard work and waiting for papier-mâché and glue to dry, your children will be ready to enjoy the puppets they have made. Set aside a time for the family puppet show. Make this a special family moment by ensuring that there will be no interruptions or distractions. Encourage the children to write an original script. Now, it's time for the children to enjoy their puppet and use imagination to create scripts and perform for friends and family.

Delight your children by becoming an enthusiastic audience for their plays. Help them make several puppets and create a whole cast of actors and actresses. If they ask for help in planning a special puppet show for another member of the family or for a special friend, give your undivided support to the enterprise.

You and your children will reap the rewards of a special time spent together making a puppet.

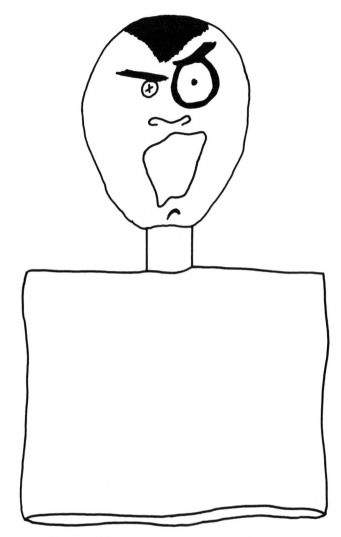

Fig. 26-3. The completed papier-mâché puppet.

Project 27

Make A
Puppet Stage

Age Group: 5 to 7
Time Required: 2 afternoons

Have you done the project in this book where you make a hand puppet with a papier-mâché head (Project 26)? It is great fun to make a hand puppet and plan a simple puppet show but, without a proper puppet stage, when the puppet performs, everyone in the audience will know that the children are running the show. Why not make a puppet stage so the children and all their wrist actions will be hidden from the audience?

A puppet stage is important for any puppet show. Waiting in front of the closed curtain, the audience grows more and more excited as the time to start the puppet show comes near. Suddenly, it is showtime and the curtain opens and the puppets appear. What fun!

Together, you and your children can make and decorate a puppet stage using papier-mâché and a cardboard box. If you have a large work area with one or two tables or countertops, you might consider working on two projects at once: making hand puppets and the puppet stage. Both projects use papier-mâché and the same common tools.

Before beginning either this project or the puppet project, explain to the children that you will have to stop before the projects are finished and then begin the work again on the day after tomorrow to allow for drying of paint. While this will sound disappointing to the children, you can keep their interest and attention by encouraging them to work with you on a puppet show idea and hold rehearsals while the papier-mâché is drying.

Your children will love having a puppet stage for their puppet performances. Through a project like this one, your children will learn a valuable lesson in working on a long-term project.

Materials and Tools

◇ Papier-mâché recipe:
  • 2 cups flour
  • 3 cups warm water
◇ Pie pan
◇ Stirring whisk or spatula
◇ Newspaper
◇ Sturdy cardboard box at least 2 feet wide, 3 feet high, and 4 feet long
◇ Piece of black felt fabric
◇ Blunt scissors
◇ Utility knife
◇ Ruler
◇ Marker or crayon
◇ Piece of string the length of the box you have chosen
◇ 3 thumbtacks or a stapler with staples
◇ Old pillowcase
◇ Needle and thread
◇ Tempera paint in three or four colors

Getting Started

Do you have a work area near a sink for easy cleanup of the leftover papier-mâché mix? Choose a work place that you will not mind getting messy. Children love mixing and using sticky papier-mache and bright tempera paints but flour, water, and paint can make a mess. Be sure and cover the table tops or counters where you will work with generous amounts of old newspapers.

Take the children and go to your local grocery store. Ask for a box large enough to hold one or two puppets. Such a box should be at least 2 feet wide, 3 feet high, and 4 feet long. Be sure the box is sturdy and has not been cut along the sides or bottom when it was opened and emptied. Ask the children if they approve of the box before accepting it. When you return home, gather your other materials and tools and go to work.

Changing a Box into a Puppet Stage

First, you must cut the top flaps from the box so they are not in the way as shown in Fig. 27-1. Sometimes this step has already been done for you at the grocery store, but if the flaps are still there, you must remove them. This is not a job for little hands because they might be harmed by the sharp cutting tool. Allow the children to watch you work.

Place the box on the floor, with the open, top side down. The bottom of the box, which is now facing up, will soon become the front of the puppet stage.

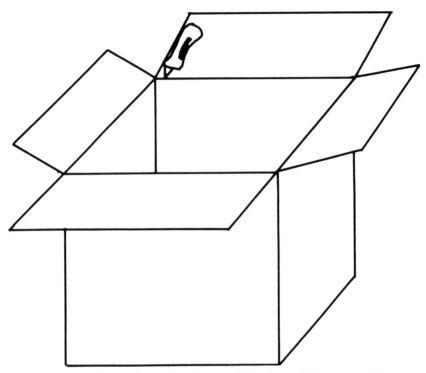

Fig. 27-1. Cut the box flaps off so they don't interfere with the puppet stage.

Help the children use the ruler and let them measure a three-inch border in from each edge of the bottom of the box. Use a marker or crayon to make a solid, dark line around this three-inch border on the bottom of the box. Again, you will have to cut the cardboard because any cutting tool would be too sharp for a child. Cut steady, straight lines. The area that you are cutting out will be the opening of the puppet stage and you and the children will want straight edges around the opening to frame the action of the puppet show.

After cutting out the center area of the bottom of the box, place the box on its side in the middle of your work area. Be sure that old newspapers cover the work area under the box. Soon you will be covering what is now the top, sides, and front (around the stage opening) of the box with newspaper strips soaked in papier-mâché as shown in Fig. 27-2.

It is time to cut some old newspapers into long, narrow strips. Let each of the children try cutting strips about 1/2 inch wide and 10 to 12 inches long from the newspapers. As they cut, have the children make a pile of newspaper strips in the middle of the table or put the strips in a box or large bowl. Keep each child's enthusiasm going by telling the hard-working paper-cutters that it is almost time to make the papier-mâché mix. Papier-mâché is really fun for children to work with.

When the children have cut one or two sections of an old newspaper into strips, let them mix the papier-mache recipe.

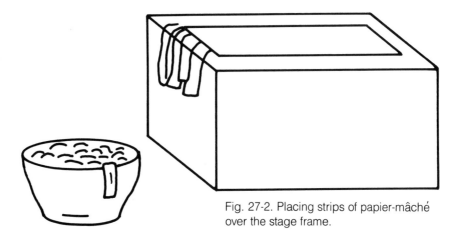

Fig. 27-2. Placing strips of papier-mâché over the stage frame.

Making the Papier-Mâché

This step offers the kind of gooey fun that makes this project one that children love. Tell the children to pour the flour and the warm water into the pie pan and mix the items together with the whisk or spatula until the mixture is thick and smooth. Do not use too much water. The newspaper strips will not adhere to the box if the mixture is too watery and thin.

When the children are finished stirring the papier-mâché mix, have them begin dipping the newspaper strips into the mix. Show the children how to apply each strip to the cardboard box.

Remind the children to squeeze the excess mix from the strips so the strips will stick and not slide from the box. Tell them to lay the strips onto the box until the surfaces of the box are covered. Once the box is covered have the children continue to place the strips on the box to form a thick layer of wet papier-mâché on the box. Be sure to show the children how to fold the strips over the edges of the stage opening that you cut in the box.

Tell the children that this layer of papier-mâché will dry out, harden, and then serve as a hard, protective surface that will allow the ordinary, corrugated, cardboard box to serve as a stage just a little bit longer than an unprotected box.

After covering the box with the layer of papier-mâché, set it aside in a safe place and allow the box to dry for about two days. Compliment the children for finishing such a long and difficult step in this project.

Making the Stage Curtain

While the box stage is drying, you and your children can make a curtain for the stage. An old pillowcase works well as a curtain.

While the papier-mâché layer is drying, measure the stage opening and add about $1/2$ inch to your measurements. Do this so that the curtain extends inside the 3-inch frame from top to bottom and from side to side.

Transfer the measurements to an old pillowcase and cut the curtain from the pillowcase. Then cut the piece of material in half so each half-piece can serve as one side of the curtain.

With the needle and thread, demonstrate how to make a tiny hem all around the edges of the newly cut portions of your old pillowcase. Fold over the cut edge and then stitch the fold of cloth.

Your children might be able to cut the pillowcase and sew the hem by themselves once they are instructed how. Encourage them to try any or all of the project steps. You can always intervene if the children seem discouraged or unable to handle a particular step. Remember, always give praise, even for an attempt to accomplish something.

Once the pillowcase curtains are hemmed, set them aside until the papier-mâché layer on the box has dried completely and has been painted.

Painting the Stage

Day after tomorrow, when the papier-mâché layer is dry, discuss with your children how they would like to decorate the stage. Again, place newspapers over the work area and gather the tempera paints and brushes to begin implementing their plan. Will your stage be painted grey and black like a rugged castle? Will it be painted in gaudy red and yellow colors like a circus wagon? Are there other decorations that the children would like to use? Let your children's imaginations determine the final appearance of the puppet stage.

After painting, the puppet stage will again have to dry for about an hour.

Hanging the Curtain

Now you can finish the puppet stage by hanging the curtain. Begin this step by running a threaded needle through the top hems of each half-curtain. Do not catch the material. Allow the curtain halves to slide along the thread.

Are the paint and decorations on the outside of the puppet stage dry? If so, turn the puppet stage so that the front of the stage (where you made the center cut, leaving the 3-inch border) is facing down on your work area. From what is now the open back of the puppet stage, reach in and place the curtain inside the front area of the puppet stage. Be sure that the string through the top hem of the half-curtains is straight along the inside of the stage front.

The threaded needle should be hanging from the top hem of the curtain. Allow one inch of the thread to hang on either side of top hem and part the half-curtains slightly so the thread is exposed in the middle also. Then, drive a staple or thumbtack over the curtain thread at each corner and in the middle along the top edge of the stage opening. Tie the hanging threads on either side of the curtain onto the staples or tacks at the right and left of the stage, and be sure that the exposed thread in the middle of the curtains is hanging over the staple or tack in the middle or is stapled securely to the inside of the stage.

Turn the box puppet stage upright and try opening the curtains from inside the puppet stage. Encourage the children to be careful when they open and close the curtains.

To finish the puppet stage, attach the piece of black felt fabric to the rear of the puppet stage. The felt will provide a nice backdrop for the puppets and it will hide the puppeteers.

The creation is finished. Now, it is time to set the stage on a table edge and let your children use their hand puppets. Position the puppet stage on a regular table or a coffee table. Have the larger rear opening along one edge of the table. The curtained front of the puppet stage should then face out over the table toward the audience seated in front of the table and stage. The children can stand behind the table and stage and easily reach inside the stage with their puppets just like Skippy is doing in Fig. 27-3. You and the other members of the audience can now sit back and let your children present a puppet show for the whole family.

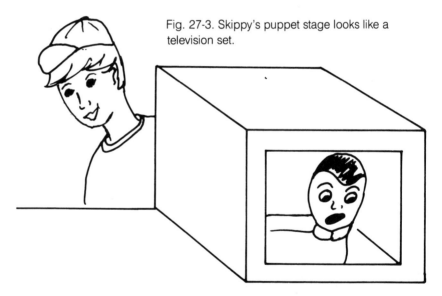

Fig. 27-3. Skippy's puppet stage looks like a television set.

The children will enjoy puppeteering so much when they have a simple stage for their puppets and plays. Encourage them to invite their friends to bring their puppets and join them in a neighborhood puppet show. The simple stage will make any show exciting.

Through puppeteering, children can learn to enjoy performing before an audience. Their confidence and creativity will grow.

Make A
Family Message Board

Age Group: 5 to 7

Time Required: 3 hours

As each of my children have grown up, I have gotten busier and busier. Now, each day, I have to remember many important appointments. One child might have basketball practice at 6:15 A.M. while another has practice at 6:45 P.M. Has a potential girlfriend called and left a message of true love? Then, there is the occasional call for my husband from a friend or business associate. How can we keep track of all this?

For as long as I can remember, keeping track of family appointments, "who called whom," phone numbers of friends, things we needed at the grocery store, appointed chores, or leaving messages so they could be found has been a constant problem. What this family needed was someone or something that could do all the keeping track and remembering for us.

Then, one day, late to pick up my daughter from swimming lessons, I desperately snatched a piece of cardboard from the trash and scrawled on it a hasty note to my husband who was due home at any minute from an out-of-town business trip, not sure if he was needed at home or if he was free to go on downtown to his office and work for the rest of the evening. I wanted him to know that he should stay home for an important call that we both might miss if we were driving to and fro. Message finished, I jammed the slab of cardboard over an unoccupied nail near the kitchen telephone and fled to the neighborhood "Y" to collect the daughter.

When I returned, I discovered hubby on the phone with the important call and additional messages from sons #1 and #3 tucked under the edge of my cardboard "note." I realized that I had come up with a solution to one type of family communications problem. We needed some type of message board and it need not be too fancy as my piece of cardboard was proving.

The board would do all those important "remembering things" for us. All we had to do was to write down things and look every day to see if there was some new thing written there.

Does your family need a message organizer for your various appointments and calls? Try this project to make a nifty little message board; then, hang it in the most traveled location of your home, and just see if it does the trick. The wonderful thing about making your own message board is that it is designed specifically for the needs of your family. The children will love creating the message board and they will be more likely to use it, too.

Materials and Tools

◇ Medium or heavy cardboard box or flat piece of cardboard at least 2 feet × 3 feet
◇ Thumbtacks
◇ Permanent colored marker
◇ Nonpermanent colored marker
◇ Cutting tool, such as a razor knife
◇ Roll of smooth, glossy white contact paper
◇ Wide masking tape
◇ Poster tape or other suitable adhesive
◇ Small calendar
◇ Ruler
◇ Blunt scissors
◇ Rolling pin
◇ 2-foot piece of string

Gathering Materials

A medium-sized cardboard box will be a good source for the stiff piece of cardboard needed for this project. Can you get a box at the grocery store? Find out when your grocery store gets food shipments. When the canned goods and other items are unpacked, there are hundreds of boxes that the store must dispose of. Just ask the manager or a clerk.

Try to take your children with you when you go to get the box. Have one of them bring a ruler or tape measure. Have the children measure the box to make sure that it will provide a solid piece of cardboard at least 2 feet × 3 feet in size. When you get home with the box, gather your tools and other materials for the project and choose a work space.

At home, have the children first measure the width of the roll of contact paper. You can make your message center just as wide as the contact paper or you can make it twice or even three times as wide. Do you have a lot of messages, telephone numbers, and appointments? If you do, you might consider making the message board twice as wide as the contact paper. After the children have measured the width of the contact paper, show them how to multiply the figure by two. If the roll of contact paper is one foot wide then have the children plan on a message board that is two feet wide.

Have the children take the measurement from the previous step and mark it on the cardboard box or sheet. Complete a rectangular area on the cardboard box or sheet by measuring a 3-foot length.

You must now use the cutting tool to cut the rectangle from the cardboard box. You must use the cutting tool yourself. Children will beg for a chance to impress you with their skills but you must keep the cutting tool up and out of the way of little hands. After cutting out the cardboard, set it aside until later.

Using Contact Paper

Have the children lay the roll of white contact paper on the table or work area, unroll it, and measure a little more than three feet along the length of contact paper. Have them draw a line across the paper and cut along this line. Give an honest compliment for a straight line drawn and cut.

Be sure that the children have placed the piece of contact paper "face down" on the work surface. The side of the paper with the adhesive backing should be facing up.

It is best that you now remove the protective paper from the contact paper as the paper has a tendency to flop, fold, and stick to itself. Generally, it can be hard to handle. The children can hold the contact paper flat and prevent it from curling.

Once the protective backing paper has been removed then hold the piece of cardboard above the sticky contact paper and properly position it over the paper so that the paper covers just one-half of the cardboard. When you are sure it is positioned, press the cardboard onto the sticky paper and fold the excess ends of the contact paper over the edges of the cardboard. Then turn it over so the cardboard is laying on the work surface.

Use the rolling pin to roll over the white surface of the contact paper now on the "up side" of the cardboard. Rolling the contact paper removes any little air bubbles that might appear where the sticky paper is not adhering properly.

Now you should have a sheet of cardboard that is exactly half covered with a smooth sheet of contact paper. Now cover the other half of the cardboard.

The surface of the white contact paper is smooth and works nicely as a tablet for writing quick messages. However, any short-term messages must be written with the nonpermanent marker so they can be erased. On the other hand, anything that you do not want to be removed must be written in permanent marker. Any messages written with the nonpermanent marker can be removed by simply wiping the surface of the board with a damp cloth.

Your basic message center is now finished. However, there are several ways you can customize the message center.

Your children might want to make a fancy border around the edge of the board with the permanent marker. Let them measure a 1-inch border around the edge of the message board. Now, help the children by placing masking tape along inside this border. When they work with the permanent marker, any mistakes will go on the masking tape and when it is removed, the message board will have a straight, neat border.

Do your children receive an allowance? Perhaps they would like to invest in an inexpensive wood or metal frame for the message center. A frame nicely finishes the project and makes it easy to hang.

Squares or strips of decorative corkboard can be added to the message center to provide a place for thumbtacks to hold photographs, school papers, invitations, special cards, or other important mementos or reminders. Be sure to have extra thumbtacks available.

If the children are able to print, have them print one of these titles at the top of the board in permanent marker: "MEMO BOARD" or "MESSAGES" or "IMPORTANT." Then, tell them to use the ruler to measure three, one-foot lengths across the message board. With the permanent marker, show the children how to make a heavy black vertical dividing line at every foot. This divides the board into three sections. Each of these sections can be permanently titled with the permanent marker. Label each of the three sections with titles such as "Messages," "Grocery List," and "Special Appointments."

Another idea might be to write the days of the week under the small calendar using permanent marker. Leave a small space between each of the written days to record chores for family members. A special appointment might need attention. Leave a large space under this section for recording these appointments. Leave another large space for writing phone messages or those special messages to mom under the appropriate section. Along the bottom of the board, leave a place to tack or tape special photographs or school papers.

Down about halfway on each of the sections, print other titles such as "Daily Chores," "Phone Numbers," and also choose a space for a small calendar. When you are finished, the board might look something like the one we made. Our family message center is shown in Fig. 28-1.

With the message board titled, divided, and possibly framed, it is time to attach the nonpermanent marker so quick messages can be written and erased. Tie a two-foot length of string on one end of a water-based, nonpermanent marker and tie a knot in the other end of the string. Push a thumbtack into the knot and then into the message board at the top right-hand corner.

Now, you and the children can hang up your family message center. Use poster tape on the back of the message center and place it on a smooth wall near the center of activity in your house. It could go in the

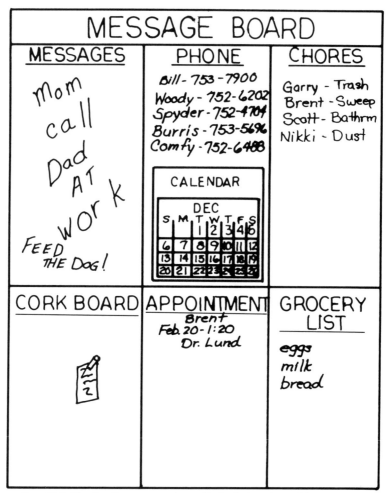

Fig. 28-1. The family message board is both handy and fun to build.

kitchen near the refrigerator or in a well-traveled hall near a telephone. Use it.

Everyone in the family will thank you for making the message board. The children will know they have performed a valuable service for the whole family. The message board is also an excellent gift for busy grand-parents, aunts and uncles, or a special friend or teacher.

Make A
Hexagonal Kite

Age Group: 4 to 7

Time Required: 2 hours

Can you imagine a March wind without a kite dancing against a blue sky? A child never running and puffing to send a kite soaring into the air? A kite and the thrills of flying one are an important part of childhood and you can help your children experience a kite.

Spring winds and kites go together and the fun of flying a kite is increased when you are flying a kite you have built yourself. A summer's day at the beach, the park, or in the back yard can also be a great kite-flying day. Then, there are fall days when warmth and sunshine linger. Who says you cannot fly a kite in the fall?

The only thing more fun than flying kites is making them, but if the kite pattern is too difficult, kite making is not much fun. This project offers a simple way to make a sturdy, colorful kite that will delight a child of any age. With simple tools and common materials, you and your children can create a kite that will provide an afternoon's fun . . . fun in making the kite and then fun in flying the kite.

We live in a perfect kite-flying spot, across the street from a huge vacant lot with no trees or power lines. Nearby is a retirement home with a flag pole always flying the American flag. Why is that important? One look at the flag tells us if today is a good kite-flying day. If the flag is stoutly waving and snapping in a strong breeze, it might be too windy for any kite. But, if the flag is placidly billowing on a gentle afternoon wind then I declare that "kite-flying weather is here." My children and I rush to find the kites stored in the hall closet and soon we are out the front door, across the street, and into the vacant lot to launch our kites.

Try making a hexagonal kite with your child. You will experience twice the thrill by seeing your own creation fly.

Materials and Tools

◇ 3 balsa wood rods or flat sticks, each 9 inches long
◇ 2 packages of white tissue wrapping paper
◇ Heavy sewing thread
◇ Sewing pin
◇ Kite string
◇ Cutting tool, such as a razor knife
◇ 7^1/$_2$ feet of kite string
◇ White glue
◇ Scissors
◇ Small hammer
◇ Pliers
◇ Ruler or tape measure
◇ Colored markers or crayons

Gathering Materials and Getting Started

A trip to your nearest shopping mall to gather materials probably will be necessary. Balsa rods or sticks are inexpensive and easily found at a hobby shop, craft store, or in the hobby section of a discount store. Balsa sticks usually come in long lengths and have to be cut to size, so take your ruler or tape measure and be sure you buy enough balsa wood for three, nine-inch lengths. The sticks can be most any width from one-quarter of an inch to three-quarters of an inch. Balsa wood rods, because they are stronger, can be any size from ^{1}/$_8$ to ^{1}/$_4$ inch in diameter.

Kite string can be found at a hobby shop, craft store, any toy store, or discount store. Just about any store with balsa wood and kite string will have tissue wrapping paper, too. Do you need anything else . . . glue, new markers, or crayons?

When you return with your materials, gather your tools and find a suitable work space.

Encourage the children to use the ruler or tape measure to measure and mark three 9-inch lengths of balsa wood. You must use the sharp cutting tool to cut the lengths from the balsa wood rods or sticks. Cutting is not a job for little hands because they might be harmed by the sharp cutting tool.

When the balsa wood is cut, have the children measure and mark the middle of each nine-inch piece of wood.

After each piece has been measured and marked, place the three pieces of wood on top of one another and, with the hammer, drive a sewing pin into and through the exact center of the stacked pieces. Refer to Fig. 29-1. If the point of the pin comes through the stack of balsa wood pieces, bend it over with the pliers to secure it in place. Then, gently spread the three balsa pieces so there are equal spaces between them.

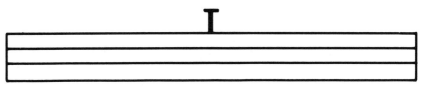

Fig. 29-1. Drive the sewing pin through the center of the stacked pieces.

 Now, with the cutting tool, you must cut a small groove in the end of each stick. Cut these grooves so you can run the heavy sewing thread through each groove and form an outline around the ends of the balsa as shown in Fig. 29-2.

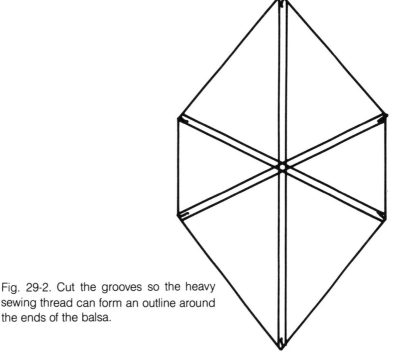

Fig. 29-2. Cut the grooves so the heavy sewing thread can form an outline around the ends of the balsa.

Tie the end of the heavy sewing thread around one of the balsa pieces and run the thread through the groove in each of the three pieces. Pull the thread tight and tie it again around the same end where you started. Tie the ends of the string together tightly.

This thread line is important because it is where you will attach the tissue paper that forms the kite, and it also strengthens the kite. Put a little glue into each groove before you lay the thread into it. This keeps the thread from slipping out and secures the thread and wooden kite frame together.

When the glue holding the thread to the balsa wood has dried, it is time to attach a "bridle line" to the kite frame. Measure and cut two pieces of kite string each 14 inches long. Tie one end of the string to one end of each of two adjacent sticks. The strings should criss-cross over the center of the kite frame.

Open and unfold the tissue wrapping paper in the center of your work area. Be sure you have a double layer of tissue paper spread out in your work area. Place the kite frame in the center of the paper. With the ruler, measure out ¹/2 inch from the thread line around the frame. Make marks or a line on the tissue paper and then cut the paper. You should now have a hexagonal piece of double tissue paper that will fit around the frame leaving a ¹/2-inch flap to fold over the thread line as shown in Fig. 29-3.

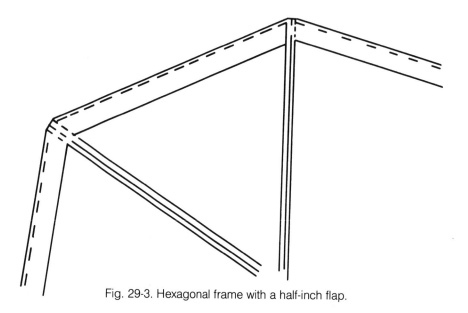

Fig. 29-3. Hexagonal frame with a half-inch flap.

Let the children color the cut piece of tissue paper. Show them pictures of fierce-looking Chinese kites from an encyclopedia. Perhaps your children wish to make the kite easy to see high up in the sky. Encourage them to color the kite in bright red, yellow, and orange.

When the coloring is finished, slip the tissue paper under the "bridle lines" and then place the tissue down on your work area with the thread and wood kite frame on top of the tissue. Center the frame and with the scissors, cut slits in the edges of the tissue for the bridle lines. Then fold the ¹/2 inch of extra tissue over the thread.

Glue the tissue securely in place, always pulling the tissue taunt. Allow the glue to dry for at least 10 minutes.

During each of these steps, your children should be able to assist you in various ways, either by holding things in position, or putting the glue on the paper.

After the glue has dried, securing the tissue paper to the thread, turn the kite over and staple a piece of kite string directly to the center of the kite where the three balsa pieces are joined. Be sure the staple secures the string and the tissue paper to the balsa wood underneath the paper. Stretch the "bridle lines" and the center line up from the front of the kite. Tie them together so they are tight as shown in Fig. 29-4. When your kite is flying, these lines will help distribute the wind forces so your kite will fly high in a strong gust of wind.

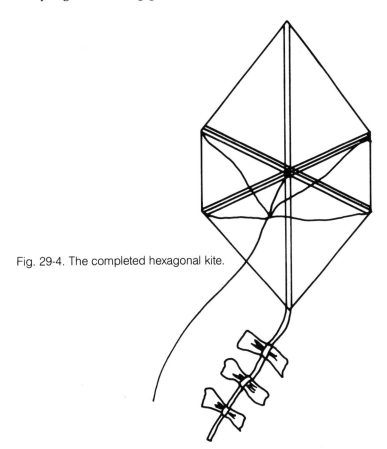

Fig. 29-4. The completed hexagonal kite.

Adding the Kite Tail

Now it's time to add the tail. The tail stabilizes the kite while you're flying it. Measure and cut another piece of kite string 7¹/₂ feet in length.

Tie the tail string to the end of the stick that will point down toward the ground while the kite is flying. Loop the tail string around the balsa wood piece inside or behind the tissue paper and securely tie the string.

Tie short lengths of tissue paper two inches apart along the whole 7½ feet of tail line. This tail with the tissue paper allows the kite to soar high into the air without dipping or diving because of the little extra weight the tail adds to the kite. If, when you launch your kite, it has a problem flying straight and steady, try adding another piece of string to lengthen the tail even more.

Your kite is almost ready. Tie the end of the kite string you will be using to the center spot where the "bridle lines" and the center line are tied together. It's time to head for the wide-open spaces. Is the wind blowing just right?

Be sure you have a safe place to fly your kite. Children, in their eagerness to enjoy a kite, will often launch it near trees or power lines. If a kite should get caught up high, children are tempted to climb into danger.

When this project is complete, you can go and make some special memories of your own just like Skippy is doing in Fig. 29-5.

Fig. 29-5. Skippy flies his hexagonal kite.

Project 30

Make A
Telephone Magnet

Age Group: 5 to 12
Time Required: 3 hours

A wonderful way to motivate children is to proudly display their art work and school papers on your kitchen refrigerator. It seems that the refrigerator is truly the center of the home and every family member opens that refrigerator door at least several times a day.

When I started displaying my "proud papers" almost 20 years ago, clear tape was my only option for hanging things. Then, those handy little "memo-magnets" came into vogue. Today, you can find all kinds of magnets that resemble miniature soda pop cans, candy bars, and common pieces of fruit.

However, there is one magnet that I have never, ever seen in a store. My sister designed a cute little early American telephone memo magnet and gave it to me. Cute little magnets add such charm to the everyday activity of posting notes, or displaying prize papers or pictures.

Do you display your children's "proud papers" or post notes on your refrigerator? Or, maybe your children are looking for a special gift to give an adult relative, friend, or teacher for Christmas, birthday, or other special occasion? This old-fashioned telephone memo magnet is easy to make and adds a special touch to any kitchen decor.

Materials and Tools

◊ Piece of wood, $2^1/2$ inches long × $1^1/2$ inches wide
◊ 2 black pushpins
◊ 2 metal thumbtacks
◊ Electrical claw
◊ 1-inch nail with small head
◊ Magnetic strips
◊ Sandpaper
◊ Old rag

◇ Clear varnish
◇ Coping saw or hand saw
◇ Small paint brush
◇ Drill with 1/4-inch drill bit
◇ Wood glue
◇ Pliers
◇ Wire cutter
◇ Damp rag

Getting Started

Gather your tools and materials for the project and choose a suitable workplace. You and your children will be working with varnish so choose an area that is well ventilated.

There are basically two kinds of tacks for bulletin boards on the market. One type is the kind with flat or rounded heads, usually metal, and the other type is often called the pushpin type with long, round plastic heads. You will use both types of tacks in this project.

The tacks with the metal heads will be used to resemble the bells on the front of your old early telephone. The pushpin type will represent the mouthpiece and the hearing piece of your telephone. The nail will represent the crank used on the old early telephones. The small electrical clamp is the type of clamp used to hold the antenna cord onto the back of your television set. The clear varnish, electrical clamp, tacks, magnetic strips, and nail are found in most hardware stores.

Search the wood pile for small scraps of wood. Measure and mark one scrap 2 1/2 inches long, 1 1/2 inches across, and 1 inch wide. Then measure and mark another piece of wood 1/4 inch thick and 3/4 inch long. The second small piece of wood is the shelf on the front of the telephone that was used on the real old fashioned telephones to hold the telephone books. Refer to Fig. 30-1 for the correct sizes.

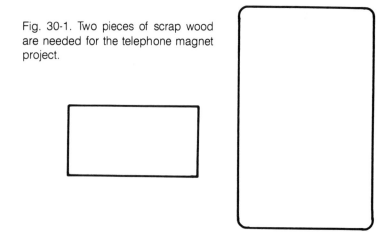

Fig. 30-1. Two pieces of scrap wood are needed for the telephone magnet project.

Older children will enjoy trying to use the jigsaw to cut the small pieces of wood. Instruct them in the proper techniques for holding and using the saw, then stand back and allow them to try to cut along the lines on the wood. Praise their efforts and step in to help if they have difficulty. When the wood is cut to the correct measurements, have the children sand the wood pieces until they are smooth and free of splinters. Then give them a damp rag to wipe the surface until it is smooth and clean.

It's time to glue the small wood shelf onto the large piece of wood. Tell the children to apply wood glue to the back end section of the smaller piece of wood and press the piece onto the lower half of the large piece of wood. Remove any glue that might cling around the edges of the small piece of wood with the damp cloth. Dried glue has a tendency to clump and leave unsightly bumps on the wood surface. Allow the glue to dry for at least 10 minutes.

Using Paint or Varnish

Spread newspaper over your work surface and prepare to varnish the small wood piece. Give your children a small, soft bristled paint brush to spread the clear varnish over the small piece of wood. Allow the wood to dry for at least one-half hour. Then tell the children to lightly sand the varnished piece with very fine-grained sandpaper. This gives the surface a very smooth finish.

Drill a small hole in the left side of the small piece of wood large enough to accommodate the end of the electrical clamp. This job might be too difficult for your children, but allow them to try if you think they can.

When the hole is drilled, place a small amount of glue into the hole then insert the round end of the electrical clamp as in Fig. 30-2. Using wire cutters, remove the point of one of the stickpins. Tell the children to push the other stickpin into the front of the telephone just above the small shelf. Above this stickpin, also push the two tacks with the round heads into the wood above and on either side of the stickpin. Refer to Fig. 30-2.

Tell the children to pound the nail into the left side of the telephone not quite half way up from the bottom edge. Then, with a pair of pliers, bend the nail up, then out. For the last touch, measure the magnetic strips to fit the back of the telephone and glue them in place with the wood glue. Hang the pushpin with the broken point into the electrical clamp and your magnetic telephone is complete.

Now you can display those "proud papers" and notes knowing that the cute little magnet is your own creation. Your friends and loved ones will enjoy receiving this special little magnet to add charm to their kitchen or bulletin board, too.

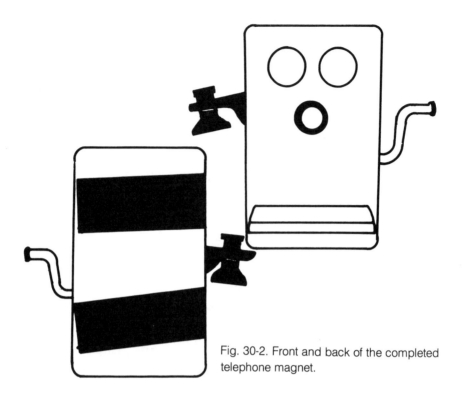

Fig. 30-2. Front and back of the completed telephone magnet.

Project 31

Make A
Walnut Strawberry

Age Group: 5 to 7
Time Required: 3 hours

Everyone wants to create a comfortable atmosphere in their home, especially in the kitchen. Special decorator touches create a homey atmosphere. How about a tiny, hand-painted strawberry to hang on the wall with other decorations? Actually, this strawberry is a walnut decorated to resemble a strawberry.

My sister must be credited with creating the first walnut strawberry I ever saw. This walnut strawberry is just one of the charming items with which she decorates her home.

You and your children will enjoy making this project just for the fun of it. In addition to its uses as a lovely decorative item, a walnut strawberry makes a wonderful gift for Mother's Day, Christmas, or any other special day. A teacher or special adult friend would love to receive a walnut strawberry from your children.

Around Christmas, you and your children can make several walnut strawberries for tree decorations. Warm, hand-made items provide such a nice contrast to electric lights and glossy decorations.

Making a walnut strawberry will provide a fun-filled afternoon of activity for you and your children.

Materials and Tools

◇ Walnut
◇ Red acrylic paint
◇ Paint brush
◇ Black, fine-line, felt-tip pen or marker with permanent ink
◇ 2-inch square of green felt
◇ 4-inch piece of red ribbon
◇ Blunt scissors

◇ Sharp cutting tool
◇ Glue
◇ Eyelet screw
◇ Black thread

Gathering Materials

Gather your materials and tools, and decide on an appropriate work area. Walnuts are easy to find in any grocery store and the other items on the list are found in any discount store. The appropriate work area must be well ventilated so paint fumes can escape.

Spread old newspapers over your work surface and be sure you are wearing old clothing. Acrylic paint cannot be removed from clothing after it has dried.

The first step to making your walnut strawberry will be to insert the eyelet screw in the top of the walnut as shown in Fig. 31-1. This is the first step because sometimes the walnut will split in half and you must begin again with a new walnut. Lightly tap the screw into the top of the walnut and turn it until only the round top of the screw shows.

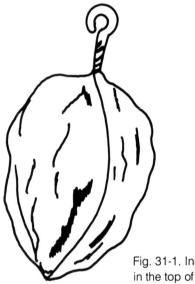

Fig. 31-1. Insert the eyelet screw in the top of the walnut.

Your children can try this procedure if you have a few extra walnuts. Otherwise, the job is best completed by an adult.

Painting the Walnut

Now ask the children to open the jar or tube of red acrylic paint and prepare things to decorate the walnut as shown in Fig. 31-2. If you have chosen to use tube paints, squeeze a little paint onto a disposable plate,

Fig. 31-2. Decorate the walnut with red acrylic paint.

such as a paper plate or piece of aluminum foil. Then have the children paint the walnut. They will love working with the bright red paint.

Wait about 25 minutes for the paint to dry.

After the children have finished painting the walnut, have them trace and cut out the pattern Fig. 31-3.

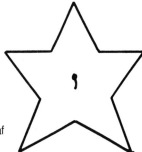

Fig. 31-3. Trace and cut out the leaf pattern using green felt.

This pattern is of the green leaf on top of the walnut strawberry. When the children have traced and cut the leaf pattern, have them lay the pattern on a small piece of green felt, draw around the pattern using a pencil or sewing chalk, and then carefully cut it out.

With the sharp cutting tool cut a small slit in the center of the leaf as indicated on the pattern piece. This slit allows you to slip the leaf over the eyelet screw. Have the children place glue on the underside of the leaf and slip the leaf over the eyelet screw. Tell them to press the leaf onto the walnut, making sure all the points are glued down securely. Wait for about 10 minutes while the glue dries.

When the glue is dry, slip a piece of red, 1/4-inch-wide ribbon through the hole in the eyelet screw. Tie the ribbon in a knot and let the ends dangle. Cut the ends so they only hang over the edge of the walnut about 1/2 inch. The ribbon adds color and charm. The children can perform almost all of this step with just a little help.

Your walnut strawberry is almost finished. All that is left are the finishing touches that make the walnut strawberry look almost real. Tell the children to use their black, fine-point permanent marker to make small

V's all over the walnut strawberry so it appears there are seeds in the skin of the walnut strawberry as shown in Fig. 31-4. These marks dry almost immediately.

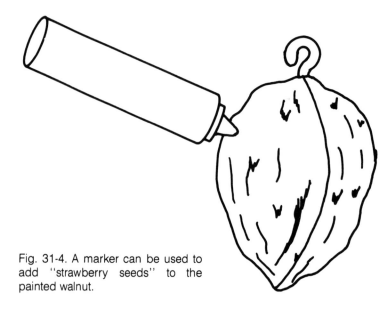

Fig. 31-4. A marker can be used to add ''strawberry seeds'' to the painted walnut.

Finally, tie a 16-inch-long piece of heavy black sewing thread through the eyelet screw for use in hanging the walnut strawberry on a nail, over a bough on the Christmas tree, or on a hook as part of a decorative display. Figure 31-5 shows a finished strawberry.

Imagine all the possible uses for your walnut strawberry. Maybe it could be used as a tree ornament for a country Christmas theme. It's a perfect gift for special times like Mother's Day, birthdays, Christmas, or even just given as a special "thank you" to someone who has done something special for the children.

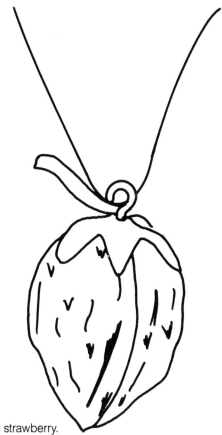

Fig. 31-5. The completed walnut strawberry.

Project 32

Make A
Scented Candle

Age Group: 6 to 12
Time Required: 3 to 4 hours

Everyone loves walking into a room filled with softly scented, fragrant air and the shimmering light from burning scented candles is also beautiful. Why not fill your home with many scented candles? Buying many scented candles is costly, but making scented candles is too hard. Right?

Wrong. Beautiful, layered, scented candles are easy and fun to make. Just follow these simple directions and, with your children, you can create a variety of beautiful decorator candles that will add much to your home. You can place one or several candles in the living room. A candle in the bathroom lends a soft light and pleasant scent to that busy room. In your bedroom, one or two candles can be quite romantic. However, candles in childrens' bedrooms can be a fire hazard, so encourage the children to enjoy making the candles while telling them about fire safety in the home.

Consider making this a family project around Christmas time to create a special family atmosphere that will bring in the holiday season. Make different scented candles for different times of the year. A deep cinnamon fragrance will be great for Christmas, while a light floral fragrance will accent the wonderful aromas of the spring season outside.

Every child in your home, large or small, will enjoy the activity and the memories of this special time together. Any child will love to give grandparents, special teacher, or friend, a lovely, scented candle.

Materials and Tools
   ◊ Paper cups to serve as candle molds
   ◊ Blocks of candle wax (paraffin)
   ◊ Old crayons
   ◊ Candle fragrances
   ◊ Wicking

◇ Scissors
◇ Paper towels
◇ Newspaper
◇ Several old cans to melt wax in
◇ Bowl of ice
◇ Pot holders
◇ Large pan of water
◇ Masking tape
◇ Pencils
◇ Clothespins

Getting Started

Gather your materials. Paraffin and candle wicking are available at most grocery stores but a hobby shop or craft store is a better source.

Any type of liquid fragrance can be added to the candle wax to make a scented candle. In addition to any fragrances for sale with the other candle-making materials, you can mix a favorite men's cologne or women's perfume with the wax.

Old crayons will provide the colors for each scented candle. When you are ready to begin this project, tell the children to collect all their old crayons. This is a good way to "recycle" the short, broken stubs of color that always collect in a child's art box. Have the children remove any paper wrappings that remain around each piece of crayon.

A kitchen table or countertop near the stove is a good place to work. Spread old newspapers over the surface of your work table or the countertop you will be using. Tell the children to place several small cans in a row on the paper-covered cabinet top. Show the children how to place several small pieces of paraffin into each can. Then have them select a different colored crayon to be placed into each can.

Have the children consider making candles that are either one solid color or candles made up of several different colored layers of wax. Use as many different cans to hold and melt as many colors as you plan to use for the layers in your layered candles.

 Now you are ready to melt the wax and crayon colors. Fill a large pan with water, place it on a stove burner, and clip the cans onto the side of the pan with the clothespins as shown in Fig. 32-1. Do not use waterless cookware because the lip on the side of the pan will be too wide for the clothespin to reach. Any narrow-rimmed pan will work well.

Turn on the stove and allow the water in the pan to come to a full boil. Watch the wax melt and take on the color of the melting crayon pieces that were selected.

If you wish to make a layered candle, have the children mark the sides of the cup to show where each different color ends and the new color begins.

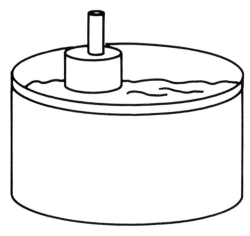

Fig. 32-1. To melt the wax, fill a large pan with water, place it on a stove burner, and clip cans onto the side of the pan with the clothespins as shown.

Cut the wicking about three inches longer than the paper cups are tall. Tape the wick onto the center bottom of the cup mold with masking tape and tie the other end around a pencil. Roll the wicking around the pencil until the pencil rests on the top of the cup as shown in Fig. 32-2. Have the children prepare a bowl of ice water and set it near the paper cups.

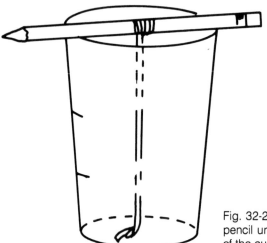

Fig. 32-2. Roll the wicking around the pencil until the pencil rests on the top of the cup.

With each cup marked and with the wicking installed, set each cup so it will be easy to fill. Be sure each cup is resting on some old newspapers just in case there is a spill of melted, runny wax.

Pouring the Hot Wax

Turn off the stove burner. After the water has stopped boiling, tell one of the older children to use a glove pot holder to carefully lift each can of melted, colored wax from the edge of the pan. Be ready to help if necessary but be patient and let the older child experience the new responsibility of handling the cans of melted wax.

Let the child pour the wax into the cup until the wax reaches the first line on the cup. Be sure to add your fragrance as you pour each layer. Now, let one of the older children place the cup in the ice cubes and submerge the part of the cup in the ice water until the wax hardens.

Let a different child pick up the next can of wax with the pot holders and pour another layer of color to the next line on the cup. Do not forget the fragrance. Again the children must submerge the cup in the ice water until that layer is hardened. They can continue doing this until each can of wax is poured to the marking lines and has hardened in the ice. When the cups are full and each layer is firm, tell the children to tear away the paper cup and cut the wick so ¹/₂ inch is sticking out of the top of the candle.

Who wants to light our first candle and enjoy the glimmering light and beautiful fragrance? A completed candle is shining brightly in Fig. 32-3.

Fig. 32-3. The completed scented candle.

If you and your children are stuck indoors on a stormy afternoon, can you think of an activity better than sharing the fun and fragrances of candle making? The children's beautiful scented candles will brighten any room and the aroma will fill the air each time you light them.

With this project, you will be creating special memories for both yourself and the children who share this time with you. A scented candle is so simple to make. Why not make several soon?

Make A Jigsaw Puzzle

Age Group: 4 to 7

Time Required: 2 weekend afternoons

My grandmother loved working on jigsaw puzzles. She loved to buy several of them at a time, and the more difficult the puzzle, the more she liked it.

You know the type of jigsaw puzzles I am talking about: 500 to 1,000 pieces covering the New York skyline at night or a blue sky full of puffy white clouds. However, the occasional puzzle was too difficult. So, she applied a little strategy to get help with her puzzle.

The difficult puzzles would appear a few days before our big holiday gatherings at Grandma's house. Grandmother would set up a card table in a corner of her living room, spread out the puzzle pieces and then leave them laying on the table partially assembled. Soon her whole house would be filled with relatives and each time someone walked past the table they would look for one more piece that might fit into that challenging puzzle. Eventually, grandmother's puzzle was completed and everyone had contributed to the project.

Most children find puzzles fascinating. I did. A jigsaw puzzle can be used to teach dexterity, reasoning skills, and attention to detail in younger children. Puzzles purchased at a book store or expensive toy shop are sometimes either too hard or too easy and always too expensive.

Why not make a jigsaw puzzle that is just right by using family photographs, school pictures, magazine pictures, greeting cards, or your children's own special drawings? These puzzles can be cut so the pieces are just the right size and difficulty for your children's ages. Besides, assembling a familiar picture is much more fun than putting together a picture puzzle from a store.

Materials and Tools

◊ Picture or drawing
◊ Ruler or tape measure
◊ Particleboard or hardboard
◊ White glue
◊ Waxed paper
◊ Rolling pin
◊ Jigsaw
◊ Newspaper
◊ Heavy old book or other weight
◊ Soft paint brush
◊ Clear decoupage finish
◊ Sandpaper

Selecting a Picture

Have the children select a picture for the jigsaw puzzle. The picture for your puzzle can be a personal photograph, a picture page from a magazine, the front of a greeting card, or a child's own drawing. To make the puzzle large enough for fun, choose a picture at least 8 × 10 inches.

If your children choose to use their own drawings, encourage them to select drawings done on unlined, lightweight, thin paper. The thinner the paper, the better it will adhere to the board.

After the children have chosen a picture for the puzzle, have them measure the picture with a ruler or tape measure. Now you and the children must locate a suitably sized piece of board. Just about any square or rectangular piece of board large enough to hold the picture will do.

For example, you might have some leftover sections of paneling that offer a smooth surface for the picture. Do you have a friend or neighbor who has a woodshop in the basement or garage? Ask for suggestions from your friend or neighbor, or visit your local lumberyard or home improvements store. You could make a simple puzzle of a few pieces from a large decoupage plaque.

Next, gather the rest of the materials and your tools for this project. Choose a suitable workplace. You will be cutting a piece of particle board with a jigsaw and some sawdust will be created. Sawdust is hard to vacuum out of a carpet, so choose a workshop, garage, or uncarpeted basement floor as your best workplace.

Have the children measure and mark the piece of wood so you can cut it to the exact dimensions of the picture. Cutting with the jigsaw is your job because using a saw is much too difficult for children. However, encourage them to watch and use this opportunity for a lesson on safety.

It is easy to use a jigsaw. Place the piece of wood on the edge of your work table and hold it down firmly with one hand while you cut along the edges marked by the children. Use easy, smooth strokes and do not rush.

After cutting the outside outline of the puzzle board, show the children how to sand the board so the surface is smooth and there are no rough edges where you cut. After they have given this job their best effort, praise them for a difficult job well done. Then you can give the board a few last licks with the sandpaper. Hand a damp old rag to your children and ask them to wipe the board clean. Any presence of sawdust can cause the picture to not adhere to the board.

Ask the children to spread a thin layer of white glue on the front of the puzzle board as shown in Fig. 33-1. A plastic picnic knife works well to spread the layer of white glue.

Fig. 33-1. Spread a thin layer of white glue on the front of the puzzle board using a brush.

Have the children position and center the picture, face up, over the glue-covered puzzle board. Cover the picture with waxed paper and roll over and over with a rolling pin as shown in Fig. 33-2. Rolling eliminates any air bubbles that might have formed in the glue under the picture. Now, tell the children to remove the waxed paper and place the puzzle in a safe place so the glue can dry overnight.

The next two steps of this project might be hard for the children to do, so either allow them to just watch or become involved by running errands. Now that the picture is securely glued on the surface of the wood, take a small, soft-bristled paintbrush and apply a thin layer of white glue or clear decoupage finish to the picture. Do you have old newspapers spread out to catch any slips or spills?

The children can do the painting, but you must monitor the process very closely because the finished surface must be very smooth with no bumps or brush lines. If you use white glue and the glue seems to be drying as you brush it on, leaving brush marks or bumps, apply more glue so you can brush it smoothly across the puzzle surface. Wait about

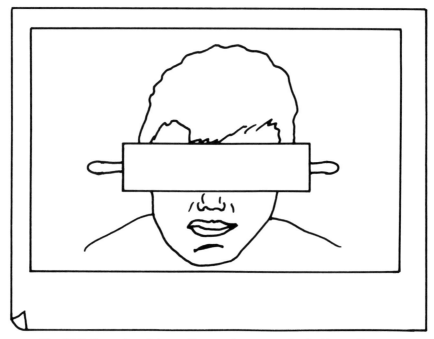

Fig. 33-2. Cover the picture with waxed paper and roll with a rolling pin.

two hours for the surface to dry, then repeat the procedure again. These thin layers of white glue or decoupage finish give the jigsaw puzzle a smooth glossy finish.

You also can use thin layers of varnish to cover the puzzle picture.

Planning the Puzzle Pieces

When the puzzle surface is completely dry, turn the board over and use a pencil to draw the puzzle pattern lines on the back surface of the board. Be sure to draw the pieces big and easy to fit together for your younger children so they can handle the pieces more easily.

If the puzzle is for older children, you can make the pieces smaller and a bit more complicated in their shapes. Cut out the pieces using the jigsaw, following your lines. Figure 33-3 shows a completed puzzle.

The puzzle you have made together is a beautiful, lasting toy your children will enjoy for years to come. Your children will remember fondly those special hours they spent with you designing and cutting this creative toy.

Fig. 33-3. An adult uses the jigsaw to cut the picture into pieces.

Project 34

Make A
Beautiful Daisy

Age Group: 7 to 12
Time Required: 2 to 3 hours

All children love flowers, especially when they can give the flowers to someone they love: mother, father, grandparents, favorite teacher, or special friend. Flowers are wonderful but, to a child, they are difficult to grow and very slow to show beautiful blossoms. On the other hand, cut flowers cost a significant amount of money to buy from a florist. If only there were some way to have pretty flowers whenever your child wanted them.

When your child wants to give a beautiful flower, now you can say something positive: "Let's make a pretty flower." After doing this project once with your children, you will soon hear: "Could we make our own pretty flowers for grandmother?"

With an investment of your time and patience, young children will be able to make not just one pretty flower but bunches of bright, white daisies. For any occasion, the children will be proud to give a loved one or friend a handmade bouquet.

In addition to the creation of beautiful flowers for little money, you will discover the thrill of fashioning these lovely flowers together with your children. Your children will be thrilled with the results and will be learning to express love by making something, rather than by spending money. To teach cooperation, teamwork, and generosity, several children can place each of their individual daisies together in one bouquet. Then, they can all share in the joy of the occasion.

Materials and Tools

◇ Colored crepe paper in light green, emerald green, lemon yellow, and white
◇ Dark green pipe cleaners
◇ White glue or paste

◊ Cotton balls
◊ Large jar lid about two inches in diameter
◊ Sheet of notebook or typing paper
◊ Blunt kitchen knife
◊ Scissors
◊ Paper clips
◊ Soft-lead pencil

Gathering Materials and Getting Started

Do you have all the materials you will need? The colored pipe cleaners and the crepe paper are available from a craft store or hobby shop. You probably have all the other materials at home.

When you have everything, begin by making the pattern pieces shown in Fig. 34-1. Encourage your child to measure the dimensions of the pattern pieces on a sheet of paper. You can help hold the paper and offer encouragement while the child concentrates on measuring and drawing the pattern pieces. Then, have the child cut the full-sized pattern pieces from the sheet of paper and set them aside in a safe place. Do your pattern pieces look like the ones shown in Fig. 34-1?

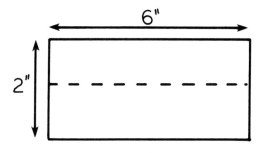

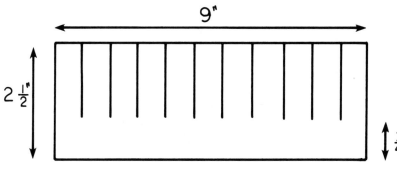

Fig. 34-1. Daisy pattern and dimensions.

For each flower to be made, place a cotton ball on the top of a green pipe cleaner. Do one as a demonstration for your child and then let the children do one. Explain that the pipe cleaner is the stem of the flower and the cotton ball will form the center of many beautiful blossoms. Later, when the children have experienced how long it takes to make one flower, let the children make as many flowers as time allows.

Let each child squeeze a cotton ball to mold it until it is the size of a pea. This step will encourage coordination. After a few moments of molding and compressing the cotton ball, encourage the children to set the cotton balls aside for now.

Lay out a piece of yellow crepe paper for each child and place the large jar lid on the paper. The jar lid should be about the size of the circle in Fig. 34-2. Help each child draw a circle on a piece of yellow crepe paper. You can steady the jar lid while the child traces around it with the pencil. Do not use a marker because it will stain the crepe paper.

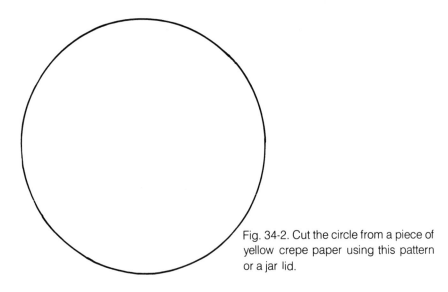

Fig. 34-2. Cut the circle from a piece of yellow crepe paper using this pattern or a jar lid.

Cutting and Gluing

If your children are mature enough to safely handle scissors, encourage them to cut the circle from the yellow crepe paper. If you do the cutting, go slowly and allow the children to closely watch how you handle the scissors. You are teaching important skills here.

Now, you and your children are ready to return to the pipe cleaner and cotton ball. Show each child how to put a small drop of glue right on top of the cotton ball. Give a compliment for a "direct hit." Glue the center of the paper circle to the top of the cotton ball. Then, gently fold and wrap the yellow crepe paper completely around the cotton ball. Before squeezing the yellow crepe paper tight around the cotton ball, put several small spots of glue at the point where the pipe cleaner goes into the cotton ball. Squeeze the yellow crepe paper around the pipe cleaner at that point so the glue holds the edges of the crepe paper. Now, the cotton ball should be completely covered with yellow crepe paper.

Using the pattern pieces, cut two strips of crepe paper in light green and yellow. Each strip should be 2 inches wide and 6 inches long. Show your children the different sides of the crepe paper. One side is shiny and the other side appears dull. Also show the children how to lay the crepe paper with the grain following the arrows on the pattern pieces.

Fold the strips of crepe paper in half as the pattern pieces indicate. Make sure the shinier side of each strip is folded to the inside.

Cut slits about 1/4 inch deep in from the folded edge of each piece of crepe paper. Then, open each one up and refold it with the shiny side out. Encourage your children to handle the crepe paper carefully. Do not crease the crepe paper.

Apply a small amount of glue to the pipe cleaner beginning just under the yellow ball. Extend the glue down the pipe cleaner for about 1 inch.

Take the folded yellow strip first and begin wrapping it around the pipe cleaner and cotton ball so that the yellow ball is nestled in the folds of crepe paper formed by the slits cut in the crepe paper. When you are finished wrapping the yellow crepe paper piece, glue the remaining edge down on top of the crepe paper so it stays tightly wrapped around your flower's pipe cleaner stem. The folds of yellow crepe paper should form a fringe around the yellow ball.

Now, apply a small line of glue around on the outside of the yellow crepe paper and wind the light green piece of crepe paper around the yellow piece. When a child has completed this difficult step, offer plenty of positive praise.

If necessary, put a few small drops of glue down between the yellow ball in the center of your flower and the yellow crepe paper wrapped around it. This will glue the center ball to the wrapped crepe paper so the flower holds together securely while being passed from grandson to grandmother or from niece to aunt.

While all the various applications of glue are drying, keep the children busy by having them cut two strips of white crepe paper about 2 1/2 × 9 inches. Again, follow the pattern piece shown in Fig. 34-1. Make sure the grain of the crepe paper follows the direction shown.

Making Petals

Now, you are ready to begin making petals for your daisy. Take one of the strips of white crepe paper and cut 1 1/2-inch slits in it as shown in the larger illustration in Fig. 34-1. Be sure to leave about 1/2 inch along the lower edge of the strip. Cut the slits about a half inch apart. Repeat this procedure with the other strip of white crepe paper. The strips of crepe paper that you have cut will form the petals of the daisy.

Wrap one of the cut pieces of white crepe paper around the pipe cleaner over the wrapped yellow and green pieces. Wrap the second piece in the same way but make sure that, as you wrap, each cut between the petals is directly over the petal underneath. This gives your daisy a realistic appearance. Does your daisy look like the daisy as shown in Fig. 34-3?

Fig. 34-3. The completed daisy.

Snip off the corners of each strip of crepe paper so it looks like a daisy petal. Do you have a book of flowers or an encyclopedia nearby so you can show the children a photograph of a daisy?

Stick the lower edge of the strip around the base as you wrap. Keep the edges even as you wrap and secure them.

Using the emerald green crepe paper, design and cut three leaves. Make sure the grain of the crepe paper is running up and down the leaves.

Again, with the emerald green crepe paper, make a 12-inch strip that is about 3/4 of an inch wide with grain of the crepe paper running across the strip.

Wrap this strip around and around the pipe cleaner, placing the leaves in the wrap at various intervals as you go. Securely glue the strip at the end of the pipe cleaner. Set the daisy aside for about 10 to 15 minutes to let the glue dry. Go treat yourself and the children to some soda pop, juice, or iced tea in the kitchen.

Finishing Your Flower

The daisy is now almost finished. To give it a realistic appearance, press open the petals of the daisy. You might want to do this yourself so that eager little fingers do not tear the crepe paper. Then, run each petal quickly over the edge of the blunt knife to curl it gently. This is definitely a job for an adult, but the children will enjoy watching. Now, the flower is finished.

Repeat these steps to make several daisies that can be placed in a simple vase. When you have finished several flowers, you will have a beautiful bouquet.

When this project is completed, you and your children will have one, two, three, four, or more white and yellow daisies. Anyone would be proud to be greeted by a beaming youngster with such a bouquet.

Make A Beautiful Leaf Plaque

Age Group: 7 to 12

Time Required: 4 hours

A leaf plaque is easy to make and requires few materials or tools. Each plaque is made from a piece of plywood 8 inches wide and 21 inches long, painted black.

A few fallen oak leaves are arranged on the black plywood, and a fine mist from a can of gold spray paint is sprayed over the leaves and, when dry, the leaves are removed. When finished, the plaques become floating autumn leaves on a field of black and gold. They are elegant wall decorations for any home.

Do you need an elegant decorating idea for an empty wall in your home? Maybe you know someone else who might appreciate a beautiful wall decoration. Present this gift idea to your children. If it meets with their approval, maybe you could make these elegant wall plaques together.

Materials and Tools

◊ 2 sheets of plywood, 8 inches wide and 21 inches long
◊ 1 or 2 small cans of flat black paint
◊ 1 or 2 small spray cans of gold paint
◊ 10 small leaves from any tree
◊ Fine sandpaper
◊ 2 narrow paint brushes
◊ 2 wall hangers
◊ Old clothing
◊ Several sheets of old newspaper
◊ Coping saw
◊ Transparent tape

Gathering Materials

Take your children on a field trip into the great outdoors and gather leaves from a tree that the children consider beautiful. Choose ten leaves all about the same size and put them in a small sack. If you want to make the field trip more interesting to the children, take along a book about the different kinds of trees in your area and tell the children the names of the trees you can most easily recognize.

Gather your materials and tools and find a suitable place to work, such as a basement storeroom or garage. Because you will be working with paint, choose a well-ventilated area so the paint fumes will not harm you or your children. Tell the children to spread old newspaper over the work area in case some of the paint splatters or spills.

Fig. 35-1. Skippy's dad helps by spraying the leaves with paint.

Getting Started

Older children might want to try cutting the scrap plywood. Show them how to hold the wood and the saw in the proper position, then stand back and enjoy their success. When the pieces of wood are cut to the correct dimensions, have the children sand the wood so they are very smooth on one side. These are the sides you will use for your painted pictures.

When the wood is prepared, have the children paint the smooth sides of the pieces of wood totally black with the black paint. Allow the paint to dry for at least 15 minutes.

Now, it is time to decorate the plaque with the beautiful leaves. Have the children lay the leaves on the plaque in various positions, winding in

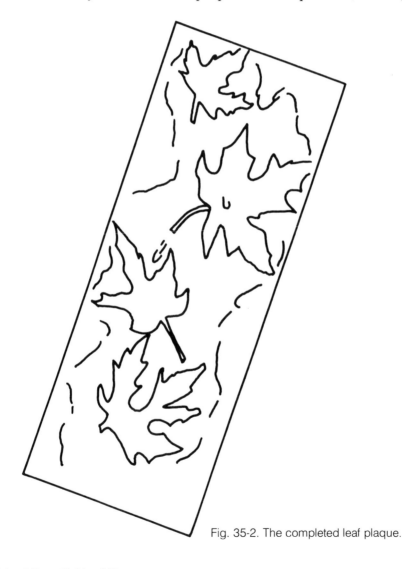

Fig. 35-2. The completed leaf plaque.

a lovely pattern down the length of the plaque. If the leaves do not stay put, place a small piece of rolled tape on the back of each leaf so they will not move.

Then lay the plaques on the sheets of old newspaper and hold the can of gold spray paint 12 to 16 inches away from the surface of the plaque you are painting. Follow the pattern of the leaves down the plaque in a quick, firm motion. The gold paint will cover the surface of the leaves and leave a scattered spray around the edges of the leaves all the way down the plaque. This step of the project requires a sure steady hand, so you might want to handle this step on your own just like Skippy's daddy is doing in Fig. 35-1.

Set aside the plaques after they have been painted and wait for about 20 minutes until they are dry. When you are certain paint cannot come off on little hands, have your children remove the leaves and discover the beautiful pattern of drifting leaves down the plaques. Figure 35-2 shows a completed plaque. You will all be pleased with the results of your combined efforts.

If you and the children choose to give these lovely plaques as a gift, someday, someone will remember you lovingly as they stand and view the plaques on their wall. Handmade gifts are always a reminder of the person who crafted them. If you choose to hang them in your own home (Fig. 35-3), you and your children can look back and remember the wonderful time you spent together making them together.

Fig. 35-3. Skippy decided to hang his leaf plaque in his room.

Project 36

Make A Fancy Photograph Album

Age Group: 7 to 12
Time Required: 4 hours

Time after time, I have entered my children's rooms to find them reminiscing about the good times of their lives while looking at old photographs of friends and family. Sounds of laughter and themes of "I remember when . . ." are repeated over and over again as they continue to enjoy past memories.

Sometimes, when fits of organization hit the children, they would gather all their cherished old pictures, written awards, and ribbons from family gatherings, school, and sports endeavors. Then they would place them in a photograph album. After this flurry of activity, the albums would be put away somewhere out of the way and forgotten until the closet was cleaned or they just had to find some important thing. Out would come the albums to be enjoyed all over again.

It has always bothered me to see the albums tucked away and periodically forgotten. Then one Christmas my children each received a wonderful, surprise gift—a beautiful photo album.

You and your children might want to try making one fancy, cloth-covered album to display your cherished pictures and memories on a coffee table or end table in the family room. Make each album with your child's name on it and have your children display them in their bedrooms.

An album is fun to make, and each one forms a unique and beautiful gift. Children, can we make one together?

Materials and Tools

◇ Standard photograph album
◇ 1 yard of cotton fabric of your choice
◇ 1 yard cotton bunting
◇ Lace for a girl's album

◇ Transparent tape
◇ Scissors
◇ Ruler
◇ School picture of the child to whom the album belongs
◇ Sewing chalk
◇ Hot glue gun and glue

Getting Started

Gather your materials and tools and choose a work space. Photograph albums are easy to find in any discount store and all of the other materials can be purchased in a sewing center. Cotton bunting used for padding in quilts also can be used for padding your album cover.

If you do not have a hot glue gun and cannot borrow one from a friend or neighbor, you might rent one from a local "rent-all" center. A hot glue gun is not an absolute requirement for this project, but using one does speed up the project process. Children should not use a hot glue gun.

Lay the material on the work table and place the open album on the material. With the sewing chalk, outline the photograph album allowing for two extra inches on the top and bottom edges of the album, and four inches at each side, as shown in Fig. 36-1. The extra material on the top and bottom edges allow for overlap, and the four inches at the sides of the album provide enough material to allow the album to open and close without stretching the material too tightly.

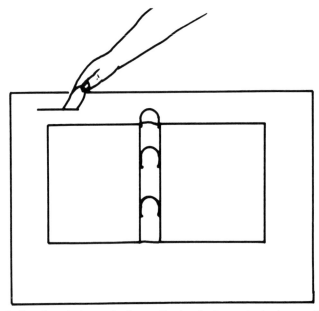

Fig. 36-1. Outline the photograph album allowing for two extra inches on the top and bottom edges of the album to the chalk line, and four inches at each side.

Next, spread out the cotton bunting. Lay the album on top of the bunting and cut the bunting to the exact size of the album.

Lay the material on your work surface, right side to the table. Center the bunting on the material and lay the album with the inside up open on the material and bunting. When you are sure the material and bunting are laying correctly under the album, snip the material so it fits snugly around the center clamp ring section on the inside of the album when the material is overlapped and glued.

Gluing the Material and Bunting

Next, apply glue, using the hot glue gun, around the inside edges of the album and lap the material over the edges onto the glue. The glue is very hot, so use two wooden spoons or other utensils to press the material into the glue.

Most 10- to 12-year-old children can do the tracing and cutting activities with your direction, but 7- to 9-year-old children might need a bit more help. If they feel they are not doing enough, remind them that doing the project together is the important part, and the time shared is valuable. They are learning to follow directions and create a beautiful, usable item.

Measure the inside areas of the album on either side of the center clamp rings, then measure the same number of inches, plus a two inch overlap on the cotton material. This material will cover the inside of the album so it will be as lovely as the outside.

Use two or three album pages as liner pages and cut them to fit the inside sections of the album on either side of the clamp. Use scissors and tape to section them together so they will fit. Lay the liner pages on the material, then wrap and glue the material around the liner pages as shown in Fig. 36-2. Remember to use the wooden spoons or other utensils to work with the hot glue so you are not burned. You can also use white glue (Fig. 36-3).

If you wish, measure the outside edge around the album, then cut lace to fit. Before the inner liner is glued to the inside of the album, glue the lace onto the inside edges using the hot glue gun. Then, glue the inner cloth liner into the album on either side of the clamp.

Decorating the Outside of the Album

Now it's time to decorate the outside of the album. Measure a 6-inch square on a thin piece of cardboard, such as a shirt box, and cut it out.

In the center of the square, draw a circle and remove the circle section from the cardboard. This cardboard square will form the frame for the child's picture.

Using the cardboard square as a pattern, cut a square of bunting. Mark out a square of printed cotton material, using the cardboard square as a pattern. Allow two inches more of the material for overlap.

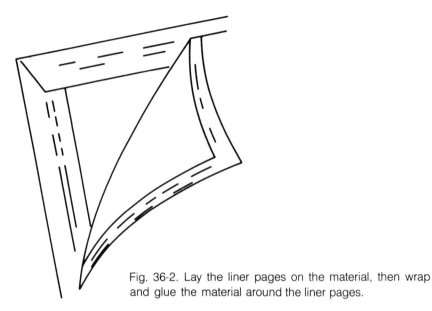

Fig. 36-2. Lay the liner pages on the material, then wrap and glue the material around the liner pages.

Draw the inside circle on the material and bunting. When the material is cut, allow for overlap on the inside of the circle. The bunting can be cut the same size as the original square because it will lay inside, under the material. If you wish, cut a lace edging the length of the outside of the square.

Glue the lace to the inside edges of the square, then glue the square onto the front upper left-hand side of the album.

The photograph album is finished. Your family and friends will spend many happy moments reviewing the contents of the lovely album because it holds pictures of loved ones and memories of wonderful times. Remember this project when you and your children want to give a lovely gift to a friend or loved one. Your children will be as proud as Skippy is in Fig. 36-3.

Fig. 36-3. You can use white glue instead of hot glue if you wish.

Fig. 36-4. Skippy is proud of his new photograph album with his own picture on the front.

Make A Kitchen Or Closet Organizer

Age Group: 7 to 12

Time Required: 3 hours

Consider making a kitchen and closet organizer with your children. The kitchen organizer is the likeness of a coffeepot cut from a piece of Peg-Board, painted with accents. The Peg-Board coffeepot holds pot holders, kitchen utensils, or any other item you might need hanging nearby your work space. The closet organizer is the likeness of a man's shoe, painted with accents. It holds belts or ties and hangs on the wall of the closet. They also make great gifts.

Materials and Tools

◇ Old clothes
◇ Small can of white glossy paint
◇ Small pieces of Peg-Board (15 inches square)
◇ 1 can of brown glossy paint
◇ 1 can of black glossy paint
◇ Decorative stickers
◇ Several paint brushes
◇ 1 can clear varnish
◇ Several Peg-Board hangers
◇ Jigsaw
◇ Drop cloth or old newspapers
◇ Turpentine for cleaning brushes and utensils

Gathering Your Materials

You can find Peg-Board and most of the other items at any lumber-yard or decorating center. The decorative stickers are found in most discount centers.

Gather your tools and materials and find a suitable work area, such as a basement, workshop, or garage. You will be using paint and varnish so be sure your work area is properly ventilated. Never work near a furnace or in any other similar area. Fire or explosion can occur when paint or varnish fumes come in contact with the pilot light of a furnace. Put on your old clothes and get ready to have fun.

Getting Started

Draw the pattern of a coffeepot or a shoe on a piece of paper, similar to the ones shown in Fig. 37-1 or 37-2. Have your children cut the pattern from the paper and lay it on one of the squares of Peg-Board. Tell the children to use a pencil to draw around the paper pattern piece so the pattern is traced onto the Peg-Board.

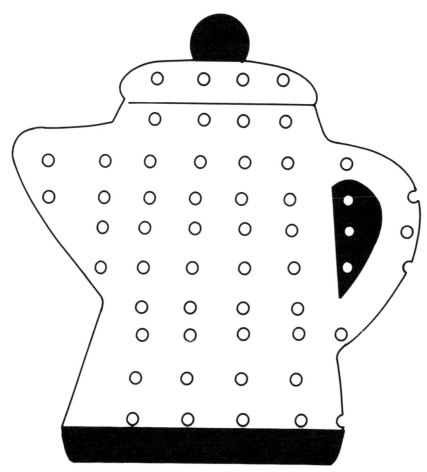

Fig. 37-1. Pattern for a coffeepot kitchen organizer cut from Peg-Board.

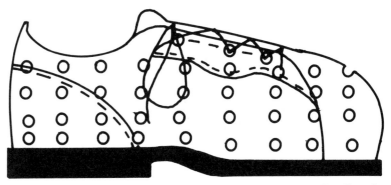

Fig. 37-2. Pattern for shoe-shaped closet organizer cut from Peg-Board.

 Ask one of your older children if they want to try cutting along the pattern lines on the Peg-Board. If they want to try, show them how to hold the Peg-Board and jigsaw in their proper positions so they are easy to handle. Have them cut along the pencil lines until the pattern appears.

When the children have finished cutting the Peg-Board patterns from the wood, they should prepare to paint. If they have not changed into their old clothes, now is the time to do so. Begin by having the children paint the smooth side of the Peg-Board white or brown, depending on which article you are painting—the white coffeepot or the brown shoe. Show them how to put the paint on in nice smooth strokes so there are no clumps or brush lines. Then lay the coffeepot or shoe on the newspaper or drop cloth and allow it to dry for about an hour.

Refer to the examples in Figs. 37-1 and 37-2 so you will know how to paint the details on the coffeepot and shoe. Use the black paint to paint a strip about 1 inch wide along the bottom of the coffeepot. Draw a place on the handle of the coffeepot that resembles a hole where the fingers are inserted when pouring the coffee. Then tell the children to paint that area black. On the top of the pot, there is a round protrusion. Also paint this part black so it resembles the handle of the lid. Make a fine brush line or use a permanent, black, fine line marker to show where the lid is removed.

Use the black paint to paint the shoe strings on the suggested location in Fig. 37-2, and also on the heel and bottom to resemble the sole of the shoe. Again, lay the articles aside so they can dry for about an hour or so. While the articles are drying, show the children how to clean the brushes. Refer to the paint can to know if you should use water or turpentine. When you are sure the articles are dry, apply the decorative stickers on the front of the coffeepot. Then tell the children to open the can of varnish and apply a thin coat of varnish to the articles. Lay them on the paper to dry again, this time waiting until the finish is not sticky. Clean the brushes thoroughly with the turpentine and put them away.

When the varnish is completely dry, turn over the coffeepot and shoe organizers and nail the wall hangers on the top back portion of the articles. Now the organizers are ready to hang.

If you and the children have chosen to give the organizers as gifts, supply wrapping paper, a box, tape, and a little instruction so they can wrap the gifts themselves. If you have chosen to keep the organizers, choose a special place where everyone is sure to see them. When someone mentions how nice they are, be quick to let them know the children worked very hard to make these wonderful organizers.

Project 38

Make A
Rubber Band Shooter

Age Group: 5 to 12
Time Required: 2 to 3 hours

On rainy or snowy days, children love challenging projects that promise a fun toy when the project is finished. Making a rubber band shooter is fun and shooting at a target with the finished toy is even more fun.

This project teaches eye–hand coordination and gives a lesson in safety. Supervision is very important while making and using this fun activity so you have the chance to spend time with your children and teach them about important concepts, such as playing safely with others.

If several children of different ages are going to do this project together, consider having one of the younger ones complete the first step of tracing Fig. 38-1. When several children work together, they all have a chance to experience team work and satisfaction. Another child can cut out the tracing and draw the outline on the piece of scrap.

Encourage the oldest child to handle the straight saw and cut the piece of wood. However, cutting with a saw is a difficult and tiring job. Be prepared to help out.

After the project is completed and the rubber band shooter is ready for use, you can organize the children for a target shooting match. Tell them never to shoot rubber bands at anyone. Shoot only at the target. Then, they will have fun safely.

Materials and Tools

◇ Wood scrap, 3/4 inch × 4 inch × 8 inch
◇ Clothespin
◇ Package of long rubber bands
◇ Wood glue
◇ Straight saw
◇ Sandpaper

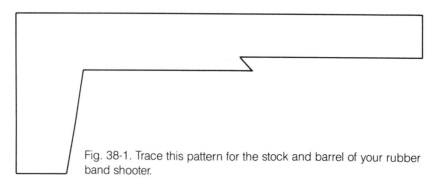

Fig. 38-1. Trace this pattern for the stock and barrel of your rubber band shooter.

◇ Tracing paper
◇ Ruler
◇ Cardboard box
◇ Magic marker
◇ Pencil
◇ Scissors
◇ Jar lids or plastic lids, several different sizes

Getting Started

Gather the materials and tools. A piece of wood scrap might be found in a basement storage room, a workshop, or the garage. Also, a piece of scrap might come from a kindly neighbor who has a wood shop.

Take a piece of tracing paper and trace the pattern of Fig. 38-1. Then cut it out.

After the paper pattern figure has been cut, lay it on the piece of wood scrap and draw around it. If several children are working on this project, let a different child do this step.

 Let the oldest child try using the straight saw to cut the wood. Direct the child to cut along the pencil drawn pattern on the wood. Be prepared to help out in this difficult step.

Sanding the Rough Wood

The rubber band shooter is beginning to take shape. It should be just the right size for small hands. However, the wood is still rough and splintery. Sand the wood so it has no rough edges or splinters.

Sanding the wood is a step that all the children can participate in. It is hard work and when one child gets tired, another child can pick up the wood and the sandpaper and continue smoothing the wood. Remind the children that teamwork is important.

When the wood is as smooth as possible, wipe the wood with a damp rag to remove the sawdust and prepare it for the next step.

It's now time to glue the clothespin to the top of the shooter with wood glue. The best way to solidly glue the clothespin is to place a layer of glue on the bottom of the clothespin and then place another layer of glue in the proper spot along the top of the shooter. Set the clothespin down in a safe place—gluey side up—and also put the shooter in a place where the glue can begin to dry without dripping. Try propping up the shooter between two coffee cups or kitchen glasses. Let the clothespin and shooter sit for about five minutes so the wood glue can begin to harden.

After the glue is set, have one of the children take the clothespin and position it in the right spot along the top of the shooter (Fig. 38-2). Be sure that the "pinching" end of the clothespin is facing down the barrel of the shooter. Watch the child do this step and be ready with a compliment. Encourage the child to press firmly to bond the clothespin and shooter together. Watch out for any drippy glue that might squeeze out from under the clothespin.

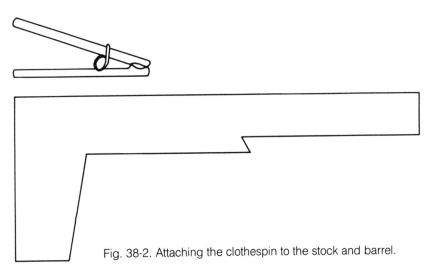

Fig. 38-2. Attaching the clothespin to the stock and barrel.

It will take about 20 minutes for the wood glue to dry. Prop up the shooter again between the two coffee cups or kitchen glasses. While the glue is drying, you and the children can make the target.

Making a Target

You can have fun target shooting with your rubber band shooter. Use a cardboard box to make the target. The best kind of box is a wide, shallow one, such as a lid from a bigger box. Take the lids of various size containers and use them as patterns for the target holes. Each child can draw a different sized circle on the cardboard using a pencil and one of the lids. Then let each child cut out one hole.

With your magic marker, write score numbers by each hole. You could give the larger holes a lower number while the smaller holes, which are more difficult to hit, could have a higher number. Let the children pick the numbers. Soon, you will have a challenging target made of several holes in various areas of the box. Now, you can help the children hang it on the wall in the family room, play area, or in a child's bedroom.

After hanging the target, measure out from the wall by taking several large steps. Place a strip of masking tape on the floor to mark a line to stand behind. When the rubber band shooter is all finished, the children can stand behind the tape line and try to shoot the rubber bands through the holes. You or another child can keep track of the points scored. Remember, the box should be your only target.

Has it been 20 minutes, yet? It is hard to wait but the glue must dry properly. You should test the clothespin to make sure it is strongly bonded to the shooter barrel. If the clothespin is securely glued, the rubber band shooter is ready. It's time to load.

Three or four rubber bands can be stored around the shooter in the area shown in Fig. 38-3, but one rubber band must stretch from the end of the shooter to the clamping jaws of the clothespin.

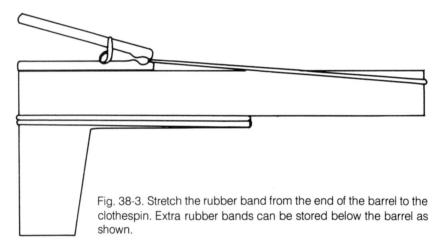

Fig. 38-3. Stretch the rubber band from the end of the barrel to the clothespin. Extra rubber bands can be stored below the barrel as shown.

You can show the children how to load the shooter by holding it in one hand and stretching the rubber band from the end of the shooter to the clothespin with the other hand. After the rubber band is secured in the jaws of the clothespin, you're ready to aim at the target and shoot. Press down on the end of the clothespin and—"snap"—you have hit the target. Safety is very important, so warn the children to never point the shooter at anyone.

When children must stay inside, their attention will be captured by this project. With this project, the children will have the chance to work with wood, a material that is always challenging fun. When you are all finished, you will have the rubber band shooter that will provide many hours of challenging target shooting in a bedroom, family room, or play area (Fig. 38-4).

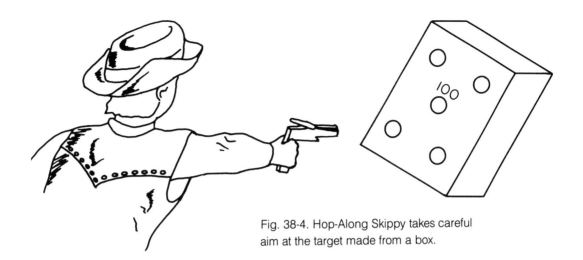

Fig. 38-4. Hop-Along Skippy takes careful
aim at the target made from a box.

Make A
Bubble Gum Machine

Age Group: 7 to 12

Time Required: 2 afternoons over a weekend

Do you experience the "gumball gimmes" every time you enter a store? Do you want to answer "yes" every time but do not because such an answer would not teach the children to be disciplined with their money? Try making a gumball machine together and reward them with a gumball for a job well done. The gumballs are inexpensive and the machine is delightful, and easy to make. The gumball machine makes a wonderful gift for your children to make with you for another child.

Materials and Tools

◇ Pint jar with a 3-inch mouth, used for canning fruit
◇ Canning ring without the center inset
◇ 8 small finishing nails
◇ 2 × 4 lumber cut into two 4-inch pieces
◇ 1 × 2 lumber about 8 inches long
◇ 2 quarter-inch, $1^1/_2$-inch dowels
◇ Electric drill
◇ $^3/_4$-inch drill bit
◇ $^1/_4$-inch drill bit
◇ Sand paper
◇ Saw
◇ Enamel wall paint (latex, enamel)
◇ Paint brushes
◇ Tape measure
◇ Drop cloth
◇ Hammer
◇ Bag of gumballs
◇ Wood glue

Gather Your Materials

If you enjoy working with wood, maybe you have wood scraps around that you can use. Otherwise, go to a lumber yard or building center and ask for a half length of 2-×-4 lumber and a scrap of 1 × 2 about eight or nine inches long. You will also find paint, nails, and a quarter-inch dowel stick at a lumber yard.

A grocery store carries pint fruit jars for canning. These jars usually come with rings and insets. The ring of the canning lid will be the top of the gumball machine that holds the jar full of gumballs.

When you have all of your materials and tools, choose a suitable, well-ventilated work shop. Spread a drop cloth or newspaper to catch paint spills and saw dust. Your work shop is easier to tidy up after the work is done if you prepare for the messy activities.

How to Make Your Gumball Machine

Lay the 2 × 4 board on your work table. If your children are old enough, have them cut the wood piece into two 4-inch sections. Examine Fig. 39-1 and cut notches that are two inches wide and a half-inch deep into the middle of the four inch section.

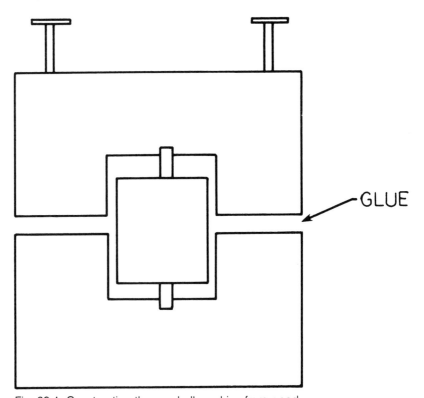

Fig. 39-1. Constructing the gumball machine from wood.

Now sand the boards and lay them aside. Prepare the 1-×-2, 8-inch piece of wood by drilling small holes through the wood at each end. The 1 × 2 is the wood slat that carries the gumballs. Use a $1/4$-inch drill bit and drill the holes in the middle of the slat $1/4$ inch away from the end. Cut the $1/4$-inch dowel stick into two, $1^1/2$-inch pieces. Push each of these small pieces into the holes in the slat. Use wood glue to hold them in place.

Have the children sand this section until it is smooth and lay it aside. Your gumball machine is ready to be painted and then assembled. Begin by painting each of the pieces with your children's choice of latex, enamel, interior paint. Wait until the paint is completely dry before assembling the machine.

STOP Fit the sections together like a puzzle before gluing or nailing it. This will assure that the slat moves smoothly through the block of wood. Then tell your children to place wood glue where indicated in Fig. 39-1 and push the wood sections together around the slat and secure the blending of the sections by driving four thin 2-inch nails into the bottom of the newly formed wood block.

Drilling the Gumball Hole

Place the $3/4$-inch drill bit into the drill and prepare to make the hole in the top of the machine. Push the slat all the way in on one side of the gumball machine and then measure $1^1/2$ inches from the front of the machine, which is the end in which the slat is pushed the furthest in. Mark your drill bit with a magic marker at two inches to prevent drilling too far into the block of wood, and stop drilling when the drill has penetrated to this mark.

At this point, set the drill point and drill into the block of wood until the drill has penetrated through the top 2-×-4 section and the 1-×-2 slat. Do a little touch-up sanding and painting to cover the marks of the drill. Your machine should look like the one shown in Fig. 39-2.

Let the paint dry.

STOP On the top of the gumball machine, place the canning ring directly in the center of the block and drive small finishing nails around the ring every $1^1/2$ inches as shown in the top view of the gumball machine in Fig. 39-3. These small nails will secure the ring so it will easily hold the jar of gumballs. Fill the canning jar with gumballs and turn the machine onto the jar until it is tightly in place. Return the machine to its upright position and slide the slat into the machine. A gumball should drop through the drilled hole into the hole in the slat and be carried out to you as you pull the slat out.

See how much Skippy enjoys his gumball machine shown in Fig. 39-4?

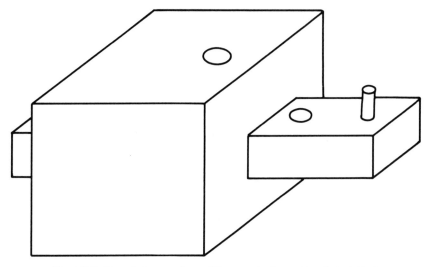

Fig. 39-2. The sliding section of the gumball machine is installed.

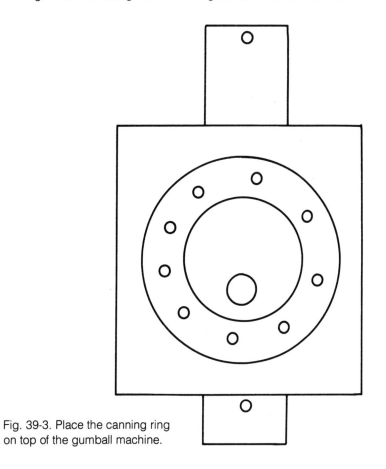

Fig. 39-3. Place the canning ring
on top of the gumball machine.

Fig. 39-4. Skippy loves the gumball machine that he helped build.

Make A
Wooden Doll House

Age Group: 4 to 12

Time Required: 1 to 2 afternoons

Role playing helps children understand what their special interests are. Children watch their mothers and fathers at work and play.

One of my favorite activities as a little girl was playing house with my neighborhood friends. We spent hours playing pretend in front of a lovely doll house, arranging the furniture and moving the dolls through the house. Sometimes we were wealthy, beautiful movie stars mourning a lost love. Other times we were mothers with small children, but always we were women decorating and keeping a lovely home. The boys of the neighborhood sometimes joined in the fun by driving their toy cars up to the doll house as they came and went from their pretend jobs. Today, little boys might pretend they were helping care for the children and home while the dolls of the girls go out to work. Children are always fascinated by a lovely miniature house.

Do your children like to pretend? Maybe they would enjoy having their own customized doll house made especially for them. If they help make the doll house, they can choose the colors and patterns for carpet, wallpaper, and outside paint. They also will learn important skills. You can teach them a few construction skills as well as patience and perseverance. The playhouse you build together will be a beautiful, lasting toy (Fig. 40-1).

This project is perhaps the most complicated of all the projects in this book. Because of the gluing and painting, it is often necessary to wait while something is drying. While doing this project, observe the children's level of interest and always be ready to change to some other activity to avoid boredom while waiting for glue or paint to dry.

Materials and Tools

◇ 4-×-8-foot sheet of $^3/_8$-inch plywood
◇ 4-×-8-foot sheet of $^1/_4$-inch plywood
◇ 3 8-foot strips of $^1/_2$-inch outside corner molding
◇ Ruler or tape measure
◇ Several pencils
◇ Sandpaper
◇ Wrapping paper
◇ Felt
◇ Double-sided transparent tape
◇ Wood glue
◇ Several cinder blocks or bricks
◇ Paint
◇ Electric saw or a hand saw
◇ Small finishing nails
◇ Hammer

Gathering the Tools and Materials

An electric band saw will make this project go much faster. Perhaps a friend, neighbor, or relative could be enlisted to help when it comes time to do the cutting. If not, you might consider renting a saw from a rental center. You should only need the saw for about an hour. Don't rent the saw until you have the plywood at home and have each plywood sheet marked so you can see what to cut.

Do you have a friend or neighbor with a pick-up truck, van, or station wagon who could drive you and the children to the lumberyard or building supply store? A vehicle with some room in it will make picking up the plywood and molding much easier. Bring the plywood home and place it in the garage or another suitable work area, such as a basement shop.

The sheet of $^3/_8$-inch plywood will be marked and cut for the floors, roof, side walls, and interior walls of the doll house. The sheet of $^1/_4$-inch plywood will be marked and cut for the back of the doll house and for the second floor windows, which are called dormers.

Once you get the plywood into your work area, lay down the sheet of $^3/_8$-inch plywood and help the children use the ruler or tape measure and pencils to mark off the following areas:

◇ The main floor: 48 inches × 16 inches.
◇ The second floor: 48 inches × 16 inches.
◇ The third floor: 30 inches × 16 inches.
◇ The attic floor: 12 inches × 16 inches.
◇ One roof half: 52 inches × 16 inches.
◇ The other roof half: 52 inches × 16 inches.
◇ Two side walls, each: 15 inches × 16 inches.
◇ Three interior walls, each: 10 inches × 15 inches.

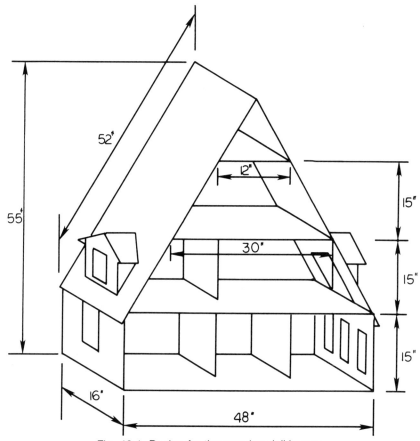

Fig. 40-1. Design for the wooden doll house.

Now, lay down the sheet of ¼-inch plywood and mark off the back wall—one piece, as shown in Fig. 40-1.

STOP Place one of the plywood sheets across sawhorses, old chairs, or support it just off the floor on cinder blocks. Using a saw, cut out the pieces of the doll house. When all the pieces are cut from one sheet, move the scraps and put the other sheet in place. Cut out the pieces marked on it.

For more detail, you can cut windows in the main floor side walls. See Fig. 40-2 for location of the windows. Also, you can cut openings in the roof sections for the dormers.

Show the children how to sand the cut pieces with the sandpaper. Smooth any rough edges where different parts will fit together. Then take a damp rag and wipe all dirt and sawdust from the pieces.

Assembling the Pieces

Place the main floor piece on a workbench or a clean spot on the floor of your work area. Spread a thin line of wood glue just next to the

Fig. 40-2. The wooden doll house will bring many hours of enjoyment today and countless hours of good memories in the years to come.

edge of the floor piece where the two side walls will sit. Spread a line of glue where the two main floor interior walls will sit. Next spread a thin line of wood glue along the bottom edge of each of the side wall and interior wall pieces.

Allow the glue to set for about 10 minutes before placing the wall pieces down on the main floor piece. Force the pieces together and quickly wipe up any wood glue that squishes out from between the pieces. Then, prop up the walls so the glue can dry and hold the walls in vertical positions. Use small bricks, scrap blocks of wood, or other objects to prop up the walls while the glue is drying. Allow the glue to dry for the length of time suggested on the glue bottle.

While the glue holding the main floor walls is drying, spread a thin line of glue along the top of each wall and allow this glue to start drying. When the glue has had about 10 minutes to set, place the second floor piece on the tops of the main floor walls. Be sure the main floor side walls do not tip when you place the second floor on top of them. Allow the glue to dry.

Next, place the back wall section of the doll house on your work surface. Spread a thin layer of glue along the edges where the floors and walls that you have assembled will fit. Apply glue to the "rear" edges of the floor/side walls section. After allowing the glue to set for about 10 minutes, turn the floor/side walls section and place it down on the back wall section where you have run the lines of glue. Place several small bricks on the floor/side walls section to press it down on the back wall section.

While the glue is drying, drive several small finishing nails through the bottom of the main floor section in the bottom edges of the various walls. Show the children how to place a nail and carefully drive it into the wood. Then let them try this step. Always be ready with a compliment or a strong hand to hold the heavy hammer.

While the glue is drying, assemble the roof, attic, and third floor of the doll house. Apply glue to the edges of the two halves and to the edges of the attic floor and the third floor sections. After allowing the glue to set, take the two roof halves and position them on the back wall section. Press the halves together and wipe up any extra glue.

Be sure that the roof precisely fits along the back wall of the doll house. While you or one of the children holds the two roof halves together, have someone slip the attic floor and third floors into position. Use small bricks or wooden blocks to prop up the walls and floors in the proper position. Allow the glue to dry.

While the glue on all the wall, roof, and floor sections is drying, begin planning the interior decoration of the doll house. Select different colors of felt fabric for carpeting. Use Christmas or birthday wrapping paper for wallpaper.

Using the dimensions of the various floors and walls, cut pieces of carpeting and wallpaper for the doll house.

To finish assembly of the doll house, place glue along the edges where the roof halves will join the top edge of the main floor side walls. Place glue along the edge where the roof halves join the back wall. After allowing the glue to set, press the roof section into position and put in the second floor wall shown in Fig. 40-1. Allow the glue to dry.

After the glue has dried, turn the doll house over on its open front so that the back wall is facing up. Drive finishing nails through the wood to secure the back wall to the main floor side walls, the roof, and the second, third, and attic floors. Encourage the children to take care in driving the nails so they do not go crooked and poke out inside the doll house. After driving the nails, your doll house should be ready for the interior decorators.

Turn the doll house up and begin placing the felt carpet sections on the various floors to make sure the fit is just what you want. Rather than gluing the carpet into the doll house, use double-sided transparent tape to hold the carpet in place. Then, when your young homemakers decide it is time for new carpet, they can easily remove the felt and put down new sections. One or two strips of transparent tape should be sufficient for each section of felt carpet.

You can use the transparent tape for attaching the wallpaper. It will stick tightly to the wood but can be peeled off when new wallpaper has been chosen by the woman of the house. When all the wallpaper and carpet has been placed, the dollhouse is almost finished. White paint can be used to paint the outside of the main floor side walls and the back wall. Flat black or brown can be used for the roof.

It is time now for the moving and storage company to deliver the furniture so the family can move in. Your children will love arranging furniture and dolls throughout the doll house (Fig. 40-2).

Index

Other Bestsellers of Related Interest

AMAZING MODELS! Rubberband Power—Peter Holland

With this book, any one can make inexpensive, working models using materials found around the house. FREE rubberbands are included! Easy-to-follow, illustrated instructions, tips and techniques are included. You'll enjoy hours of fun. 64 pages, Illustrated. $7.95 paperback only

SO YOU THINK YOU'RE SMART—150 Fun and Challenging Brain Teasers—Pat Battaglia

Put on your thinking cap and delve into this delightful book of "brain games." These games are easy to understand, uncomplicated, and strictly nontechnical (no mind – bogglin math!). There are no trick questions—all the puzzles are completely straightforward and logical. Most of these brain teasers are word games; a few involve elementary logic, but most of them just require good common sense. 96 pages, 43 illustrations. Book No. 3106, $7.95 hardcover only

MODEL CAR BUILDING: Getting Started—Dennis Doty

In *Getting Started*, the basics of model car building are thoroughly covered. Chapters include a rundown of the tools and materials you need, descriptions of various painting methods, and details on realistic finishing applications for both plastic and metal car assembly. A brief history, tracing model cars from the introduction of $1/16$ – scale wood models in the '40s to large – scale models popular in the '70s is given. The making of a model kit, from the proposal stage to actual assembly and testing in the manufacturer's shop, is followed. 128 pages, Illustrated. Book No. 3085, $7.95 paperback only

THE TOOLS OF SCIENCE: Ideas and Activities for Guiding Young Scientists—Jean Stangl

Providing science experiences that will stimulate children's curiosity and motivate them to explore and discover the world around them is a challenge for adults today. This book is an excellent course for teachers, parents, and youth leaders looking for fresh ideas. Jean Stangl has taught both children and teachers for over 25 years. This extensive experience is evident in this delightful book that will create hours of educational fun for elementary school children. 160 pages, 26 illustrations. Book No. 3216, $8.95 hardcover only

MARIONETTE MAGIC: From Concept to Curtain Call—Bruce Taylor, Illustrations by Cathy Stubington and Bruce Taylor

Puppets are fun weekend projects and offer a welcome challenge to the woodworker who is seeking a change of pace. Requiring no prior puppetmaking experience, this book provides a complete apprenticeship in puppetmaking, as well as a concise course in staging. Taylor describes how you can transform wood, plaster, and papier – mache into animated figures. Complete plans and detailed instructions are accompanied by tips and tricks of the trade. 176 pages, 143 illustrations. Book No. 3091, $12.95 hardcover only

DYNAMITE KITES—30 Plans to Build and Fly—2nd Edition—Jack Wiley and Suzanne L. Cheatle

Dynamite Kites—30 plans to Build and Fly can introduce you to the fascinating hobby of kite building. Complete plans, instructions, and illustrations for making a variety of kites are presented from very old designs to more recent innovations. The revised second edition offers an improved instruction format and greater simplicity. Projects are easy to follow and clearly diagrammed. Although no prior knowledge of kite building or kite flying is presumed, there is a kite project here for every level of interest and building skill. Go fly a kite! 140 pages, 70 illustrations. Book No. 2969, $8.95 paperback only

YEAR-ROUND CRAFTS FOR KIDS—Barbara L. Dondiego, Illustrated by Jacqueline Cawley

Easy to use, the handy month-by-month format provides a year of inspiring projects, many focused on seasonal themes to ensure young children's enthusiasm. Valentines, paper airplanes, and cookies for Easter, paper bag bunny puppets, string painting, Hanukkah candles and gingerbread boys, bell and candle mobiles and of course Christmas trees for December are just a few of the fun things to make. 256 pages, 180 illustrations, plus 8 color pages. Book No. 2904, $12.95 hardcover only

200 ILLUSTRATED SCIENCE EXPERIMENTS FOR CHILDREN—Robert J. Brown

An ideal sourcebook for parents, teachers, club and scout leaders, or anyone who's fascinated with the wonders of science, this outstanding book is designed to make learning basic scientific principles exciting and fun. Literally crammed with different and interesting things to keep your youngsters entertained for hours, the collection of experiments presented here demonstrated such principles as sound, vibrations, mechanics, electricity, and magnetism. 196 pages, 200 illustrations. Book No. 2825, $8.95 paperback only

THE WORLD'S GREATEST PAPER AIRPLANE AND TOY BOOK—Keith R. Laux

With *The World's Greatest Paper Airplane and Toy Book*, you can transform a simple sheet of paper into a creation capable of flight! This is a complete manual on the art of paper airplane folding. Forty different aircraft designs are presented. Ten toy designs are also included. 120 pages, Full illustrated. Book No. 2846, $6.95 paperback only

CRAFTS FOR KIDS: A Month-By-Month Idea Book—Barbara L. Dondiego

Creative and educational crafts for small children designed by a professional! More than 160 raft and cooking projects that can be made easily and inexpensively, from readily available materials! Step-by-step instructions plus exceptional illustrations enhance each project which are arranged by months to take advantage of special seasonal occasions! 224 pages, 156 illustrations. Book No. 1784, $11.95 hardcover only